Reclaiming the Bible

Reclaiming the Bible

Words for the Nineties

Robert McAfee Brown

Westminster John Knox Press
Louisville, Kentucky

© 1994 Robert McAfee Brown

Book and cover design by Drew Stevens

Cover illustration: The Beatitudes *by Marina Silva. From* The Gospel in Art by the Peasants of Solentiname, *ed. Philip Scharper and Sally Scharper. Reproduced by permission of the Burckhardthaus-Laetare Verlag GmbH, Geinhausen/Berlin, in collaboration with Jugenddienst-Verlag, Wuppertal.*

First edition

Published by Westminster John Knox Press
Louisville, Kentucky

This book is printed on acid-free paper that meets the American National Standards Institute Z39.48 standard. ∞

PRINTED IN THE UNITED STATES OF AMERICA
94 95 96 97 98 99 00 01 02 03 04 — 10 9 8 7 6 5 4 3 2 1

Library of Congress Cataloging-in-Publication Data

Brown, Robert McAfee, 1920–.
    Reclaiming the Bible : words for the nineties / Robert McAfee Brown. — 1st ed.
       p.   cm.
  ISBN 0-664-25553-1 (alk. paper)
    1. Presbyterian Church—Sermons.   2. Sermons, American.
I. Title
BX9178.B7425R46   1994
252′.051—dc20   94–8687

To the Members of
First Presbyterian Church
Palo Alto

They Endured

Contents

Prelude: A Funny Thing Happened on the Way to the Pulpit   ix

Part 1. Recovering a Vocabulary   **1**
1. Mystery: Where Questions Count for More than Answers   3
2. Theology: Loving God with the Mind   9
3. Lost and Found: Grace, Amazing   16
4. That Much-Abused Word "Love"   22
5. Liberation: Cliché or Rediscovery?   27
6. Reversals, Reversals, Reversals   33
7. Reconciliation: The Bottom Line   39

Part 2. Exploring a Terrain   **45**
8. The Official and Unofficial Reports of a Lower Echelon
   Functionary in Herod's Court (Advent)   47
9. Three Messengers (Which Is What the Greek Word *Angelos*
   Means) Discuss Past and Future Assignments (Epiphany)   53
10. The Biblical Obsession with Food (Ministry)   59
11. Mary and Martha: A Conundrum (Ministry)   64
12. "So What Happened Next?" (The Transfiguration)
    A Dialogue Sermon with Sydney T. Brown   70
13. Holy Week according to CBS and NPR, or Dan Rather
    and Robert MacNeil Cover the Jerusalem Beat
    (Palm Sunday and Good Friday)   76
14. The Life and Times of Old Tom Didymus (Easter)   83
15. The Apocryphal Council of Alexandria (Trinity Sunday)   89

viii

Part 3. Confronting a World   **93**

16. "How Shall We Sing the Lord's Song in a Strange Land?"   95

17. The Spiral of Violence   102

18. Sexuality and Homosexuality: A Problem for the Churches   109

19. Scandal, Justice, Pearl Harbor, and Other Related Items, Including "a Refiner's Fire"   115

20. Sacrifice—and the Federal Budget   122

Part 4. Coda: Death and Life   **129**

21. Giving Thanks in the Midst of Death?   131

22. Dear Mackenzie: A Letter from the Depths   138

Notes   145

Prelude: A Funny Thing Happened on the Way to the Pulpit

Most of my "professional" life, a seminary degree notwithstanding, has been devoted to teaching rather than preaching. My sanctuary has been the classroom, my pulpit has been the podium, and my liturgies have run the gamut from class discussions to blocking draft board entrances. Whatever preaching I have done, therefore, save for a brief stint as a Navy chaplain and an even briefer stint as Acting Dean of the Chapel at Stanford University, has almost always consisted of one-shot appearances—a quick entrance and a quicker exit, leaving the host pastor to pick up the pieces.

So when Diana Gibson, our pastor at First Presbyterian Church, Palo Alto, California, asked if I would help by preaching about half-time while we were looking for new staff, I didn't say "yes" automatically. When I finally did, it was after making two commitments to myself: (1) no warmed-over old sermons and (2) consistent use of the lectionary.

The first promise was surprisingly easy to keep. Perusal of even a few of those old sermons made clear that they belonged permanently in a file drawer, never again to be exhumed. The decision to use the lectionary led to a surprising liberation rather than a threatened confinement.

Early on, I made a freewheeling survey of the congregation on whether or not I should follow the lectionary: 12 percent answered, "Yes," 23 percent answered, "It's up to you," and 65 percent answered, "What's the lectionary?" The lectionary, I tried to explain, is an ecumenically created collection of four readings for each Sunday, spread over a three-year cycle. Each week provides a reading from the Psalter, the Hebrew Scriptures, the Gospels, and the Epistles. Take your pick.

The challenge to preachers is to choose from among these readings and build a biblically oriented sermon that speaks to where folks are today. The advantage to everyone is that the preachers must expose themselves to more than their small collection of favorite biblical texts ("the canon within the canon," as we call it in the trade), and attempt over a period of time to expound *the whole range* of biblical material. Sometimes the selections open up beautifully into a theme that speaks to one's given time and place. Other times it is the very devil to discover anything that seems worthy of attention. But I would report that only once in three years did the lectionary let me down; that was the weekend after the verdicts in the Rodney King trial, when the force of contemporary circumstances pushed me back to the book of Amos, with its stern message of judgment and its demand for change.

The pages that follow, then, are sermons. Let there be no dissimulation on that score. If I sound defensive, it is because the notion of "printed sermons" has always seemed to me (save in the hands of a great preacher) to be at best a second-degree oxymoron: sermons are to be heard, not read, and they are addressed to specific people in a specific time and place. Their hallmark is the relation of the Bible to *the particularity of the here and now*. True enough. But I also learned during those three years (1990–93) that the particularities of the here and now turn out to be pretty universal as well: death, war, insecurity, doubt, joy, sexism, grace. So I ask readers, when it is necessary, to transpose my here-and-now situation into yours: Joan's death, your son's involvement in the Gulf War, your own insecurity about job loss, the erosion of your faith into doubt when a nephew gets AIDS, joy in the birth of your first daughter, the undermining of your self-worth by sexism in the workplace, along with, however frequent or infrequent, the experience of grace.

During the three years when I was preaching these sermons, our congregation was sustained by the love and commitment of many persons, but most of all by the love and commitment—and courage—of our pastor, the Reverend Diana Gibson. I express my personal gratitude to her for what her ministry meant to me, as I was trying to engage in ministry with her.

R.M.B.
Palo Alto, California
1990–93

Part 1
Recovering a Vocabulary

Many words in the Christian vocabulary fail to communicate any-more to non-Christians, let alone to Christians. Some of them have had their day and should be allowed to disappear. (Words like "double predestination" and "supralapsarian" come to mind.) But the central concern of this part is not iconoclastic. As far as pos-sible we should try to recover the best of the "old" vocabulary, drawn largely from scripture. A unique message needs a unique vo-cabulary. Consequently, Part 1 is an attempt to rehabilitate some of the great words of our tradition, without which we are limited in our ability either to hear or to speak the Christian message in its fullness. Any list could be considerably longer, but the words dis-cussed—mystery, theology, grace, love, liberation, conversion, and reconciliation—are at least some of the essential words we need to reappropriate.

– 1 –

Mystery: Where Questions Count for More than Answers

Reading: Exodus 33:12–23
Text: Moses prayed, "Show me your glory." . . . The Lord said, "I shall cover you with my hand until I have passed by. Then I shall take away my hand, and you will see my back, but my face must not be seen."—Exodus 33:18, 22–23

The lectionary reading comes from an early period in Jewish history. The Israelites have escaped from Egypt and are in the desert, hoping to end up someday in what they call "the promised land." They have come to Mt. Sinai, and despite the disastrous episode of the golden calf, the Ten Commandments have been transmitted to them through Moses. In the passage we will read, Moses and God are negotiating terms for the rest of the journey. Will God continue alongside them or not? What signs will there be of God's presence? Moses is particularly interested in establishing impressive enough credentials of divine support to be followed in the future. Can't God be just a little clearer about the whole business?

Moses said to God, "You tell me to lead up this people but you have not told me whom you will send with me. You have said to me, 'I know you by name, and, further, you have found favor with me.' If I have indeed won your favor, then teach me to know your way, so that I can know you and continue in favor with you, for this nation is your own people." God answered, "I will go with you in person and set your mind at rest." Moses said to God, "Indeed if you do not go in person, do not send us up from here; for how can it ever be known that I and your people have found favor with you, except by your going with us? So shall we be distinct, I and your people, from all the peoples on earth." God said to Moses, "I will do this thing that you have asked, because you have found favor with me, and I know you by name."

And Moses prayed, "Show me your glory." God answered, "I will make all my goodness pass before you, and I will pronounce in your hearing the name Jahweh. I will be gracious to whom I will be gracious, and I will have compassion on whom I will have compassion." But God added, "My face you cannot see, for no mortal man may see me and live." God said, "Here is a place beside me. Take your stand on the rock and when my glory passes by, I will put you in a crevice of the rock and cover you with my hand until I have passed by. Then I will take away my hand and you shall see my back, but my face shall not be seen." (Exodus 33:12–23)

This is a curious and primitive story, in which the imagery for God is that of a person (a male person, I'm afraid we'll have to concede, in faithfulness to the text) with hands and arms, a front and a back, with a permanent address on a mountaintop in the Sinai peninsula, conversing, presumably in Hebrew, with a leader of the people. There has already been enough griping and unrest about God so that the leader, Moses, wants some hard data to take back to the people demonstrating that his credentials are authentic and that the God with whom he purports to be meeting is really God. And so there comes the importunate and almost plaintive plea, "'Show me your glory.' Let me know who you really are. Dispel the mystery."

But the mystery is not to be dispelled. Moses will not be permitted to see the divine glory directly. He will, however, be permitted to see its traces, God's back, after God has passed by. And that's all. The mystery will remain a mystery.

A quaint story, yes, but really, the imagery being set aside, a very modern story. Who among us when we reflect about God, would not like more clarity? "Put up or shut up," we want to say when something mysterious hovers around the edges of our lives. "If you are really there, show us. If not, leave us alone." Which serves only to heighten the mystery, for why should we be disturbed by something that isn't there?

I

The starting point for the religious quest is always a confrontation with mystery. That's not a self-evident truth. For centuries the church has proclaimed that the starting point is God, that there are assured things we can know about God, and that if we will just believe them, our confusion will be dispelled. Now to be sure, as we persevere in our religious quest, we discover that if there is a God, God got there first, long before we did, long before we knew anything about him—or her. And we will see our gropings and our stumblings and our halfhearted commitments as somehow being held within, and even guided by, the divine mercy. But that is a conviction we arrive at only in hindsight, farther down the road than most of us have yet gotten. So let's agree for the moment that *we start with mystery.*

And here, even if it initially sounds a little pedantic, we have to make an important linguistic distinction or we'll get it all wrong. The distinction is one between a *mystery* and a *problem* handily summarized by Gabriel Marcel, a French Catholic existentialist. A *problem* is something "out there," that with the help of a little ingenuity, and maybe luck, we can solve, and thus dispose of. Problem: how do we get a man to the moon? Answer: we engage in years of research, test theories and models, anticipate difficulties and figure out how to overcome them, build a spacecraft and launcher, and, sure enough, we get there. We have solved the problem.

Such an approach works pretty well for many objective tangible areas of life, but it doesn't work so well when we consider our hopes and fears. We talk quite wrongly, for example, about the problem of evil, a reality that threatens every life many times over. If evil is really a problem, then we can in principle solve it, figure it out, do away with the causes, and finally eliminate it from the scene. All power to those who can cut down on the incidence of cancer or Alzheimer's or airplane crashes. But after all the successes, evil will still be around as an ineluctable part of our lives, never to be fully overcome. For evil is not a problem; it is a *mystery.* We must try to understand it as well as we can, but we will never fully do away with it. It is a mystery within which we live, whether we like it or not, and about which, when it confronts us, we do certain things in response: get angry, complain, seek to lessen evil's scope, lose our faith, and sometimes confront it with courage and seek to draw something good out of it. But it remains a mystery.

We can see this more positively if we consider not only the mystery of evil but the mystery of love. Why do two people fall in love? No matter how much we know about glands, genes, common interests, or sexual attraction, love is never a problem we solve and put behind us, but a mystery within which we live, and we can live increasingly rich and full lives to the degree that we affirm the mystery. Woe to the one who, when asked, "Why do you love so-and-so?" can immediately reply, "Well, there are three reasons. First . . ." That won't do. Nor, if the love is real, will we be able to account for, in strictly rational terms, the reasons we behave the way we do:

Why are you sticking so close to the phone these days? (She might call.)

How come you are suddenly so absentminded these days? (I'm thinking about him.)

Why the sudden rush for the mail? (She might have written.)

What's with all the new dresses? (He or she likes to see me in new clothes.)

It is *never* the case that the more we know about mystery the less mysterious it becomes. Quite the contrary: the more we know about mystery—

of evil or love or anything else—the more the sense of mystery heightens. She gets to know you better and better and discovers what a mediocre character you really are under all that cultivated veneer, *and she still loves you.* The fine edge of mystery.

Tony and Polly will soon be celebrating their fiftieth wedding anniversary. How do people make it together for fifty years? Don't look for three crisp answers. It's a mystery, a holy mystery, and the more we enter into it the more wonderful and complex—and mysterious—it becomes.

II

So if mystery is the starting point, what is the nature of our response, especially when we are dealing not only with human mysteries but with the divine mystery as well?

1. Our initial response, if we are to be authentic about mystery, is *silence*. Take to heart the words of the Advent hymn "Let All Mortal Flesh Keep Silence." The mystery, whether human or divine, is so awesome that we can't be glib about it without cheapening it. I am intrigued as a theologian (and remember that speech is the bread and butter of a theologian's existence) that two very different contemporary theologians—Dietrich Bonhoeffer of Germany and Gustavo Gutiérrez of Peru—independently arrive at this conclusion. "Teaching about Christ begins in silence," Bonhoeffer wrote, and then cited Cyril of Alexandria, "In silence I worship the unutterable." And Gutiérrez says that "theology is speech that has been enriched by silence." Just as two people in love are finally reduced to silence, so the love that God offers can finally be received only in silent gratitude. Later we respond aloud, but first we respond in silence.

2. When we begin to speak, our speech, if it is authentic, will be *reticent*, even halting. There is nothing less convincing than the individual who knows everything about God and is only too willing to describe the heart of the divine mystery, which thereby becomes mystery no longer. Distrust the TV evangelist who knows exactly what God's will is, particularly the amount of money God wants you to send to the evangelist as soon as the program is over. I recently heard a sermon by a minister who knew all about God, thanks to what he called "the three omnis": God is omnipresent, God is omniscient, God is omnipotent; God is everywhere, God knows everything, God is all-powerful. Got it? You are fully in the know. Hold on to the three "omnis" and nothing can threaten your faith.

The early Christians were more linguistically circumspect and realized what a chasm there is between God and what we can know of God. They employed what came to be called the *via negativa* (the way of negation) to talk about God, claiming that while we can never know who God *is*, at least we can know something about who God *is not*, and one of our modern hymns "Immortal, Invisible, God only Wise" has caught the flavor. God is "immortal," not mortal; God is "invisible," not visible. Further on, God dwells in "light inaccessible hid from our eyes." God is "unresting, unhasting, . . . nor wanting, nor wasting." There is a deep authenticity in such reticence.

3. Behind silence and reticence lies *wonder*, the deepest response to mystery—wonder at how extraordinary, how beyond anticipation, how amazing, is all that lies at the heart of mystery. In Alice Walker's book *The Color Purple*, Celie (the narrator) and Albert (the husband who has never loved her) finally come to the beginnings of reconciliation in face of mysteries they cannot dispel. Albert says to Celie:

> I start to wonder why us need love. Why us suffer. Why us black. Why us men and women. Where do children really come from. It didn't take long to realize I didn't hardly know nothing. And that if you ast yourself why you black or a man or a woman or a bush it don't mean nothing if you don't ast why you here, period.
>
> So what you think? I ast.
>
> I think us here to wonder, myself. To wonder. To ast. And that in wondering bout the big things and asting bout the big things, you learn about the little ones, almost by accident. But you never know nothing more about the big things than you start out with. The more I wonder, he say, the more I love.
>
> And people start to love you back, I bet, I say.
>
> They do, he say, surprise.

To be filled with wonder is to listen to the mystery of Gregorian chant, to know we can't really explain it, to realize that it touches the deepest part of who we are, and to be grateful for that, surrendering ourselves to the mystery and letting the music weave its spell of wonder around us. Or it is to be given the gift of forgiveness when we know we don't deserve it, and having the grace to accept it without ever expecting to understand it.

There are many words here—wonder, awe, amazement (one of Rabbi Abraham Heschel's favorite words to describe the human condition when touched by grace), reverence, even a certain kind of fear. (It was Elie Wiesel who said, "Whenever an angel approaches you and says 'Fear not!' you'd better start to worry—a big assignment is on the way.")

4. There is still another response to mystery, as Albert in *The Color Purple* discovered. In the face of mystery we are encouraged *to ask questions*. We may not have a lot of answers but we have a lot of good questions. We know

what they are: Why do people suffer? Does God suffer too? Can we trust the one who is at the heart of mystery? Where do we get the energy to keep going? How are we going to keep from blowing up the planet? What are we supposed to do with the unexpected gifts we have been given?

My sister and her husband had to confront the tragedy of the death of their only son. And she, wrestling with the blow, confided to her next-door neighbor, who was Jewish, "If I ever get to heaven, I'm going to line up before God's throne and demand, 'Why did this happen? Why did you let this happen?'" And he, out of the heritage of centuries of unjust Jewish suffering, responded immediately, "Hattie, it's a very long line."

It is, and it ought to be. Like Job on the dung heap, like Jeremiah in exile, like Jesus on the cross, we are permitted, even urged, to voice our complaints, just as on other occasions we voice our gratitude.

III

There are many ways in which we can respond to the mystery that surrounds us. Among all the questions we ask, there will surely be one that goes something like this: Granted that, like Moses, we will not see the full glory at the heart of mystery, where can we situate ourselves so that we can at least see what would be analogous to the "back" of God? Where are the little hints, the pointers, the direction signals that say, "Yes, you are getting closer to, rather than farther from, the heart of the mystery"?

The short answer is that mystery need not remain the equivalent of an indistinct oblong blur. For there is a claim—the most astounding claim of all—that at the heart of mystery is love, better yet, grace (which is love that is undeserved and yet given anyhow). It calls us, if we want to understand it better, to live grace-filled lives, to be vehicles through whom the love and grace of God can move out to others whose lives intersect with ours. And the good news is that it can embrace all that we do—how we treat our children, what kinds of demands we place on our politicians, how we spend our time on the job, how we react to precarious situations, and all the rest.

Of course there is a longer answer as well that we must explore. But not in this sermon.

O God, you confront us as mystery, and you give us opportunities to respond to your mysterious presence. Help us to work through in our own lives what that means, to look for traces of your presence in unexpected places, to hear your voice in the voices of friends, to see your purposes in the opportunities you open up before us, and in the life of Jesus of Nazareth, who gives us our surest clues, and in whose name we pray. Amen.

– 2 –

Theology: Loving God
with the Mind

Reading: Mark 12:28–34; Matthew 22:28–32
Text: You must love the Lord your God with all your heart, with all
your soul, with all your *mind*, and with all your strength, [and]
you must love your neighbor as yourself.—Mark 12:29–31, (italics added)

During the last week of Jesus' life, his enemies in Jerusalem kept plying him
with questions, hoping that they could trick him into a self-incriminating comment. One of them, not mincing words, asks the basic question, "What is the
first of all the commandments?" Jesus, who knows perfectly well what is going on, takes an unassailable position, quoting the *Shema Yisroel* ("Hear, O
Israel. . . ") from the book of Deuteronomy, the basic summary of Jewish faith.
For good measure he throws in a second commandment, which is really another way of stating the first.

The questioner is impressed, reiterates his own understanding of the theme
Jesus has highlighted, and he, in turn, elicits Jesus' approbation.

There are probably a dozen sermons lurking within this classic exchange, all
but one of which will have to be postponed for another occasion.

> Then one of the scribes, who had been listening to these discussions and had
> observed how well Jesus answered, came forward and asked him, "Which is
> the first of all the commandments?" He answered, "The first is, 'Hear, O
> Israel; the Lord our God is the one God, and you must love the Lord your
> God with all your heart, with all your soul, with all your mind, and with all
> your strength.' The second is this: 'You must love your neighbor as yourself.'
> No other commandment is greater than these."
>
> The scribe said to him, "Well said, Teacher. You are right in saying that
> God is one and beside God there is no other. And to love God with all your
> heart, all your understanding, and all your strength, and to love your neigh-
> bor as yourself—that means far more than any whole burnt offerings and sac-
> rifices." When Jesus heard how thoughtfully he answered, he said to him,

"You are not far from the kingdom of God." After that nobody dared put any
more questions to him. (Mark 12:28–34)

At a seminary that shall remain nameless (both to protect the innocent
and because the story is apocryphal) a graduate returning for his fortieth
class reunion happened to see the final exam in systematic theology that
had been given just the day before. To his astonishment he discovered that
the exam was identical with the one he had taken forty years ago. "Don't
you ever change the questions in the theology exams?" he asked the pro-
fessor of systematic theology. "No," came the response, "we don't change
the questions anymore, we just change the answers."

Now that's both appalling and appealing: appalling since it suggests
that statements about Christian faith are unsteady and unreliable, able to
reflect only the most current linguistic fads; but also appealing, since it
suggests that there might be more than one way to state the truth, that
words change their meanings, and that new vocabularies may be necessary when old vocabularies wear out.

But is that a problem for anybody but seminary graduates? Surely other
people don't need to develop theological distinctions or bone up on linguistic skills as part of trying to live the Christian life. Right?

Wrong. For this somewhat forbidding word "theology" points to something that is everybody's business. Coming from the Greek, like so much
of the rest of our Christian vocabulary, the first part of the word, *theos*, is
the Greek designation for "God," while the latter part, *logos*, means "word"
or "discourse." So theology quite literally is discourse about God, words
about God, or, most succinctly, God-talk. Whenever you talk about God
you are being a theologian. You may not be a very good theologian, or, on
occasion, you may be a brilliant one, but whatever you say about God is a
theological utterance. You may call God "the all-cohesive source of reality," suggesting that God is some sort of cosmic glue, or you may say, "God
is like Jesus, only more so," at least giving your hearers something to think
about. But whatever you say, you'll be a theologian.

So let's have no nonsense about theology coming only from *my* side of
the pulpit to yours. Every statement about why you are a Christian, every
"call to act," every prayer of intercession or thanksgiving, expresses a theological conviction.

As Jesus put it, to highlight the portions of the text on which we will
focus, "You must love the Lord your God with all your . . . mind." Not just
heart, soul and strength, but mind as well. Paul tells us on one occasion to
be ready always to give an accounting of the faith that is in us, to share

with others what we believe, to engage in God-talk. How do we go about it? How do we love God with the mind? Three proposals:

I

First of all, *we start where we are*. The tools at our disposal all come from life immediately around us. If we want to speculate about divine love, that love is somehow stretched out of whatever we know about the best of human love. If we want to talk about God's forgiveness, whatever we affirm will be extrapolated from what we know of human forgiveness. When Jesus wanted to talk about God's realm, he didn't offer a lecture on metaphysics, he dug his convictions out of the soil of human experience: God's realm is like a woman who loses a coin (read "her Social Security check") and looks everywhere for it; like a shepherd who has lost a sheep and goes out into the night to find it; like a group of bridesmaids preparing for the moment when the groom will appear; like a person who sees a pearl of great price in a field and buys the field in order to possess it. Ordinary, usual stuff—lost and found, weddings, business deals—but the best handle we have on what turns out to be *extra*ordinary and *un*usual stuff.

We have a check on whether our speculations are off the wall or not; we can compare our human images with the images offered by other folks. The image of the church as "the pilgrim people on the march" is a human image we discover in the letter to the Hebrews; Jesus as "liberator," one who frees us up, is an old human image that has been given fresh currency by Christians in Latin America, Asia, and South Africa; that our salvation— our wholeness—comes not from our good works but from our acceptance of God's grace, is a human image Martin Luther bequeathed to us out of his own struggle with despair, one that he in turn had found in Paul, who got it from Habakkuk, who got it from the psalmist.

Starting where we are also means starting with our questions. Job directed a lot of questions at God. So did Jeremiah. So do we. Such questions as, Why do the righteous suffer? Why do the evil prosper? How come you let all that happen, O divine ruler of the universe, eh? Those are honest questions, not just abstract theological conundrums. They are even more honest when they come out of our own experience: Why did my child die? How come my competitor can cheat like crazy on capital gains and never get caught? Why are we peacemakers so often at the mercy of the warmongers? Why does my partner have AIDS and yours doesn't?

What we do, from our human starting point, is to keep pressing the questions and making use of as wide a gathering of resources as we can muster. To Protestants, that has been one of the great values of the Bible.

The Bible poses all those questions and many more. It doesn't give easy answers, but insists that we get into the story and take part in it also. And as we do so, we discover that some of the wisdom of those old characters, some of their faith, even some of their courage, rubs off on us.

Roman Catholics have a more clearly defined sense of tradition, the "correct" way to reflect on their faith, and that can be a further help. But also, as many contemporary Catholics are finding, it can be a tremendous burden, since so many of the claims appear to be leading them away from the truth rather than toward it—a problem, we Protestants better add in all candor, that we frequently have with the Bible. This ambiguity of theological argument, Karl Barth reminds us, goes right back to creation. Eve's real problem, he says (not totally tongue in cheek), was not all that business about the apple but that she made the mistake of getting into a theological discussion with Satan.

II

In addition to starting where we are, *we need to keep our theological claims modest.* That's not too hard for those of us whose theological convictions are not exactly robust. But we need to be aware of the temptation to claim too much for whatever theological convictions we do arrive at. Christians are always tempted to latch onto a *part* of the truth and claim it as the whole. We experience God's love, and can't conceive that a God who loves might also frequently need to be stern with us. Or we feel ourselves so indicted by God for some wrongdoing that we can't image anything beyond that bad news.

Historically, we Presbyterians have often been accused—and found guilty—of claiming too much for our human theological utterances. We were among the most compliant participants when fundamentalism first appeared on our shores. But there is a beautiful example of theological modesty, and its self-correcting possibilities, in one of the early statements of our Scottish forebears—a disclaimer in the Scots Confession, written over four hundred years ago:

> . . . protesting only [the Scots divines assert] that if any persons will note in this our confession any article or sentence repugnant to God's Holy Word, that it would please them of their gentleness and for Christian charity's sake to admonish us of the same in writing. And we upon our honor and fidelity, by God's grace do promise unto them satisfaction from the mouth of God, that is from Holy Scripture, or else reformation of that which they shall prove to be amiss.

Taking this confession of human fallibility seriously, the Presbyterian Church in our own time adopted a new confession of faith, the Confession of 1967. It was initially meant to replace a much earlier and formidable document, the Westminster Confession of Faith (1647), concerning which it had become clearer and clearer over the decades and centuries that if it is true that the Holy Spirit guards and protects the church, it must be acknowledged that the creation of the Westminster Confession was an occasion when the Holy Spirit guarded the church with only minimal zeal. However, those entrusted with the task of creating a new confessional statement decided that instead of just replacing an old confession with a new one they would offer a collection of confessional and creedal creations from various times in the church's history, two from the early church, four from the Reformation (including the Scots Confession), and two from the present.

The intention behind this move was not to dilute the faith, but precisely to exalt it, by insisting that no single human construct could ever fully explicate the faith, and that it would be better, therefore, to offer a variety of pointers toward what we believe. All confessions are conditioned by the times and cultures in which they were created, so that no one of them can claim to be the absolute truth. Consequently, we are never to dot all the *i*'s, or cross all the *t*'s of any human statement, but let those statements together *point toward* the living truth that no single one of them can ever fully grasp.

A succinct handle on this principle is articulated by the Oxford historian Herbert Butterfield, who said creatively, if a bit dangerously, "Hold fast to Christ, and for the rest be totally uncommitted." He was seeking to remind us that our faith is not faith in a system, or a theological formulation, or even a historic confession, but faith in *a person*, a living reality. Hold fast to that person, he is saying, and don't make any exaggerated claims about the trappings that have come to surround that person. Faith is not a formulation of the intellect but a relationship of personal trust. To trust that God's love for us is enacted in the life and death and resurrection of Jesus of Nazareth counts for more than having a correct doctrine of the two natures of Christ, or an impeccably orthodox formulation of the atonement.

III

That suggests a final comment on how we engage in theology, and without it we can end up in a huge trap of our own devising. *We need to take seriously the move from God-talk to God-walk,* as Fred Herzog characterizes it.

During the same hectic week in Jerusalem that we were examining a few moments ago, Jesus tells a parable: Two sons are ordered by their father to work in the vineyard. One son replies, "I'll go and do as you ask, sir," with a ring of assurance in his voice. But he flunks the test. He doesn't go. The somewhat gutsy but rash other son, says in effect, "Hell no, I won't go." But he passes the test because, as Jesus says, he "changed his mind" and went, after which Jesus adds an alarming postscript that we'll come to in a minute. Question: Which one did the father's will? Answer: No contest; the one who actually went, no matter what either of them said.

Transfer the concerns of that episode to our own situation. One person says, "I believe we are all created in God's image," and then within the hour engages in Japan bashing because Toyotas are outselling Chryslers. Another person says, "If you really want to know the truth, I don't believe in God," and then knocks herself out to see that Laotian children are not discriminated against in the local fourth grade, where there have been rumors of trouble. Where does the truth lie? In the *deed*, not in the words. You really *don't* believe Japanese are made in God's image (no matter what you say) if you bash them; you really *do* believe in God (no matter what you say) if you are sensitive to the needs of the least of God's children.

So our theology isn't finally communicated by what we say, no matter how orthodox the statement or how well we enunciate, it's communicated by what we do, no matter how unexpected the deed.

In the '60s, a popular expression for this sort of thing was "enacted speech." If you blocked a draft board you might not be saying a single word, but you were communicating a very clear message by your action: young Americans should not be drafted to go and kill young Vietnamese. That was enacted speech, what today is sometimes called body language.

So authentic theology is more act than utterance. I have nothing against utterance (having made my living off it for over forty years), but if someone wants to know what our theology is, he or she will know better by our deeds than by our words. Real theology, to return to Fred Herzog's image, is not so much God-talk as it is God-walk; not so much trying to talk about God as to walk in God's footsteps, to do God's will. Which is a pretty tall order.

Jesus puts it less gently: if we are among those who say, "We'll go," and do not, those whose speech is denied by their deeds, Jesus states categorically that the tax collectors and prostitutes will make it to the kingdom of heaven long before we do. End of discussion.

That, of course, is why we finally need the *whole* text of the passage from Mark. To each of us, Jesus says you must not only love God with your heart, mind, soul, and strength, you must also, to give those words any authenticity, love your neighbor as yourself.

That's *real* theology.

O God, we offer up our words to you for whatever they are worth. We know that actually they aren't worth much. But we ask you to accept them as our gift to you, and then empower us so that with your help we may continually narrow the gap between what we say and what we do. Help us to find better words, but even more than that empower us to do stronger deeds. In Jesus' name we pray. Amen.

– 3 –
Lost and Found:
Grace, Amazing

Reading: Philippians 2:1–13

This morning's lectionary reading is notable not only as one of the most important single passages in the New Testament, but because of the circumstances of its composition: Paul is writing from prison. In doing so, he set an example for later generations of Christians: John Bunyan's *Grace Abounding to the Chief of Sinners,* Martin Luther King, Jr.'s *Letter from a Birmingham Jail,* and Dietrich Bonhoeffer's *Prisoner for God: Letters and Papers from Prison.*

Although being in prison is never an experience to anticipate with relish, Paul argues in the first chapter that things have really fallen out rather well, since he has been able to reach a whole group of people—both jailers and fellow prisoners—whom he would otherwise never have encountered. When one is in prison, one's faith is stripped down to its bedrock realities, and these Paul points out in the passage we will hear: an opening section about the demands our faith makes on us, a second section on how God actually deals with us, and a final short section on how we are supposed to respond.

> If then our common life in Christ yields anything to stir the heart, any loving consolation, any sharing of the Spirit, any warmth of affection or compassion, fill up my cup of happiness by thinking and feeling alike, with the same love for one another, the same turn of mind, and a common care for unity. There must be no room for rivalry and personal vanity among you, but you must humbly reckon others better than yourselves. Look to each other's interest and not merely your own.
>
> Let your bearing towards one another arise out of your life in Christ Jesus. For the divine nature was his from the first; yet he did not think to snatch at equality with God, but made himself nothing, assuming the nature of a slave. Bearing the human likeness, revealed in human shape, he humbled himself, and in obedience accepted even death—death on a cross. Therefore God raised him to the heights and bestowed on him the name above all names, that at the name of Jesus every knee should bow—in heaven, on earth, and

in the depths—and every tongue confess, "Jesus Christ is Lord," to the glory of God the Creator.

So you too, my friends, must be obedient, as always; even more, now that I am away, than when I was with you. You must work out your own salvation in fear and trembling; for it is God who works in you, inspiring both the will and the deed, for his own chosen purpose. (Philippians 2:1–13)

Once upon a time the Brown family spent the fall and winter academic quarters at Stanford-in-France. There were about eighty sophomores of all shapes and sizes—a few practicing Catholics, a few lapsed Catholics, a fair number of Protestants, mostly lapsed, a group of Jewish students in varying degrees of acceptance and rebellion from their tradition, and a sizable contingent of what the theologian Friedrich Schleiermacher called "religion's cultured despiser," whom I designated as "happy pagans." (France turned out to be a culture in which pagans could be deliriously happy.)

Until one day during the field trip to Italy, when a member of the group was in a motorcycle accident, and after being in a coma for two weeks, died. As the resident religion prof I was asked to work out with a few students a kind of informal memorial service, which we held the evening we got word of Richard's death. Given the heterogeneous character of the group, I bent over backward to avoid being sectarian or even Christian, so that *all* the students, at whatever place they were coming from, could participate without reserve. It went well.

At its conclusion, however, nobody left. It was clear that we still needed time with one another. One of the students went up to her room and returned with a guitar. After we sang a couple of songs out of the '60s (from which we had scarcely emerged), to my great surprise she started playing "Amazing Grace," and to my even greater surprise, everybody—lapsed Catholics and Protestants, secular Jews and not-so-happy pagans—all joined in. And somehow the words of that very sectarian, very Christian hymn filled a vacuum in those students' lives. I had been wrong to be so timid in avoiding such expressions of belief. The student guitarist knew better. There was somehow a universal need in that group to give testimony to the reality of *grace*.

I

If mystery is the starting point in the religious quest, we soon have to entertain the possibility that at the heart of mystery is not a void, not darkness, not nothingness, but grace, creative outgoing love that accepts us as we are and offers to help us rebuild our lives. Not just hints, but a flat-out

claim that what the word "grace" points to is the bedrock Christian affirmation, on the truth or falsity of which the truth or falsity of our lives as
Christians rests.

How can one begin to talk about so momentous a reality? All one can
do is dance around the reality, content to grasp after a few things rather
than many things. Let our guide for that improvised choreography be the
portion of Paul's letter to the Philippians that we have just heard, which,
although it does not contain the specific word "grace," is really about
nothing else. Happily for homiletical purposes, the passage falls into three
distinct sections.

The first four verses present a staggering agenda of what God calls us to
be and do. We are to have the same "warmth of affection or compassion"
for others that God has for us (v.1). We are to have "the same love for one
another" that God has for us (v.2). Nor does Paul equivocate about what
this will mean specifically: "There must be no room," he writes, "for rivalry
and personal vanity among you, but you must humbly reckon others better than yourselves. Look to each other's interest and not merely your
own" (vv. 3–4).

Now that's a beautiful dream sequence or fantasy. But as a series of
marching orders for this afternoon and tomorrow morning? Lots of luck.
Anyone in his or her right mind knows perfectly well that we won't come
even close to such a goal, and other words of Paul will rise up to describe
us with considerably greater accuracy: "The good that I would, I do not,"
he confides to the Christians in Rome, and even more honestly and alarm-
ingly, "the evil that I would not, that I do" (Rom. 7:19).

It doesn't matter whether we call that condition sin, or the existential
predicament, or the human situation, or missing the mark. It's *where
we're at*, when we are honest with ourselves. (And if you don't, on some
level of your being, feel yourself described in that acknowledgment of
Paul's, feel free to daydream through the rest of the sermon: none of it
will make any sense.)

II

But suppose that *is* where we're at. And suppose we don't know where
to go with it. We've discovered that we can't pick ourselves up by our own
moral bootstraps and suddenly make ourselves do all those things Paul
expects the Philippians to do. We *don't* feel "the same warmth of affection
or compassion" that God does, maybe even toward some people in the
same pew, and we *don't* really "reckon others better" than ourselves, in-
stantly flashing on those crummy people at the office who are trying to do
us in.

What then? Well, there's a rumor that there is good news as well as bad news, and good news, we need to keep reminding ourselves, is exactly what the Old English word "gospel" means in modern English. And it's on good news that Paul dwells through the balance of the lectionary passage. The nub of it is this: what we can't do for ourselves God does for us. Rather than demanding that we ascend to the divine heights, God descends to the human depths, right where we are. Paul asserts that God enters directly into our own situation, as one of us, takes the burdens of humanity off our shoulders, and frees us up for a new life in which God will guide and empower us.

Now if the first part of Paul's message is, as described, a staggering *agenda*, this second part is a staggering *claim*. We should never cease to be surprised by it. We should never take it for granted. We should never try to "tame" it or reduce it, so that it loses its amazing character. It is a description of "amazing grace." In Jesus, Paul says, one who was "in the form of God," gave all that up, assuming instead "the form of a slave," shared our human lot, even to the point of dying like we do (in his case a more gruesome death than most of us will experience). He did all that to show the measure of God's love, and the depth of God's commitment to us. It was God's reckless gamble that we are salvageable material.

There is a wonderful example of this in Lorraine Hansberry's play, *A Raisin in the Sun*, about a black family in Chicago that is finally going to be able to move out of the slum. But the son squanders the money, so that nothing is left but the down payment. The family, needless to say, dumps on him hard, until finally the mother says, "Has anyone of you shed a tear for him, knowin' how awful he feel about what he done? We ain't supposed to love him just when things is going good; we supposed to love him when he's way down at the bottom."

That's a beautiful human parable of divine grace. That's what grace is— God hanging in with us, whether we deserve it or not, loving us no matter how unlovable we may be, and refusing to give up on us, no matter how discouraging it may become.

On any ordinary human calculus, that kind of tenacious love makes no sense. It's a losing proposition. We don't deserve such treatment. Yet, on any divine calculus, it is the very meaning of grace, as Samuel Crossman puts it, in a hymn we will examine on another day: "love to the loveless shown that they might lovely be." When we accept it, we are in a brand-new situation. Good news, as our children say, "good news to the max."

III

Thus far Paul has shown us what we are supposed to do—and do not, and what God promises to do—and does. And that throws the ball back into our court. How do we respond to God's response?

One long-standing response has been to leap onto this particular theological bandwagon on the assumption that it gives us a dandy out. In "For the Time Being," W. H. Auden puts on the lips of Herod a classic response to this kind of unconditional love: "Every crook will argue: 'I like committing crimes. God likes forgiving them. Really the world is admirably arranged.' " That's not just a line Auden dreamed up for a quick laugh. Whenever Paul talked about grace, he got a similar response: "Well, if what you say is true, let us sin boldly that grace may abound. The more sin, the more grace."

Of course, that's no true response to grace even on a human level. That's being exploitive rather than responsive. If you lie to your best friend, and she forgives you, your authentic response is not, "Wow! I can keep on deceiving her because I'll always keep on being forgiven." No. The response has to go something like, "She's giving me another chance, when I don't deserve it; I'll try to be worthy of her trust this time."

Paul Tillich has described how a proper response to God's grace begins. He understands grace as acceptance, and the message of grace as being, "You are accepted," even if (and especially when) you deem yourself unacceptable. The good news is that to God you are never unacceptable. So the basic message is "Simply accept the fact that you are accepted."

Now I believe that is deeply true. But it is only the *beginning* of a full response. For if grace is *gift*, grace is also *demand*. When grace is offered to us, one of the ways we accept it is not to clutch it, but to be a vehicle through whom it is passed on to others, whom we are to accept even when they seem "unacceptable."

The final portion of Paul's letter picks up this theme. We are, Paul says, "to work out our salvation with fear and trembling," but not alone, for "it is God who works in us, inspiring both the will and the deed, for [God's] own chosen purpose." That intermingling of divine grace and human freedom as a favorite—and complex—Pauline theme: "I, yet not I, but the grace of God within me," he says on another occasion in describing this new divine-human relationship. Let us be reminded that being a recipient of grace is not the end of the road. We are to be *channels* of grace as well. And the good news here is that we are freed up to be such channels and to act in the world. We don't have to worry about our status before God anymore. That has all been taken care of.

Are we really worthy of God's love? Probably not, but we are loved anyhow. So our job is to make the love that we have received spill over into how to relate to other people, how we use our time, how we vote, how we best express our concerns about the Gulf crisis or the Bosnian crisis or whatever crisis stares us in the face at the moment. A grace-filled life, then, is lived outward toward others. Deeds of action are as much the fruit of grace as prayers of petition and thanksgiving. Neither is sufficient without the other.

IV

What is the appropriate way to conclude a sermon on grace? The great Christian affirmations are always best expressed in song, and are always communal rather than individual. The students in France had the right idea. Affirming the words of "Amazing Grace" is an initial step on the road to the reality of grace that John Newton wrote about. Who was John Newton? Listen:

John Newton, after what he called a profligate youth, became a slave trader in his more mature years. He was converted to Christianity by reading Thomas à Kempis's *The Imitation of Christ* during a storm at sea on one of his slave-carrying vessels, and became an Anglican clergyman. Rediscover the words of his hymn (printed in the notes at the end of this book). In line two he calls himself bluntly a "wretch," which is a degree of self-designation that most of us resist. What the designation points to, however, is part, though by no means the only part, of a description of who we really are *in addition* to being made in God's image. (How to balance being a wretch and being made in God's image is one brief way of stating the Christian agenda.) Because of grace, John Newton tells us, the wretch is no longer a wretch. He *was* lost, but he *is* found (just like the sermon topic says). He was blind—blind to the image of God in black African slaves, for example—but now he *sees*, sees the image of God in those same black African slaves, who therefore are no longer merchandise, nor can John Newton traffic in slave trading any longer.

In the second verse we see that grace first induces "fear" in the author as he saw who he truly was and how deep was his need. But then grace his fears "relieved," as he discovered that God's mercy was stronger even than John Newton's sin. He acknowledges in verse three that he is still on journey, and will be for the rest of his life, but once having tasted the reliability of grace, he knows that the gracious God will never let him go. So:

> The Lord has promised good to me,
> His word my hope secures;
> He will my shield and portion be
> As long as life endures.

So be it for us all.
    Amen.

– 4 –

That Much-Abused
Word "Love"

Reading: 1 John 4:7–12
Text: Love to the loveless shown that they might lovely be.—From
the noncanonical writings of Samuel Crossman (1624–1684)

Tucked away in the back of the New Testament, a region into which we seldom venture, is a series of three short letters—one of them less than a single printed page—called the Johannine letters. We do not know who wrote them, though the style bears some resemblance to the Fourth Gospel, likewise attributed to someone named "John." They appear to have been written around the end of the first century, seventy years or so after Jesus' death. But authorship and date are not as important as the message, which circles around the words, "Little children, love one another."

The lectionary reading is from the first of these letters. It offers a summary of the Johannine message, and indeed of the heart and center of the Christian message as a whole.

> My dear friends, let us love one another, because the source of love is God. Everyone who loves is a child of God and knows God, but the unloving know nothing of God, for God is love. This is how God showed the divine love among us; God sent a Son into the world that we might have life through him. This is what love really is: not that we have loved God, but that God loved us and sent a Son as a sacrifice to atone for our sins. If God thus loved us, my dear friends, we also must love one another. God has never been seen by anyone, but if we love one another, God's very self dwells in us; God's love is brought to perfection within us. (1 John 4:7–12)

If you were challenged to state the heart of the Christian message in ten words or less, what words would you choose? Ten words are not very many, and even "Johnthreesixteen" fails the test since it contains eleven words. My own conclusion (after conducting biased surveys on this question for forty years) is that we would be hard put to come up with a better summary of our faith than the second line of "My Song Is Love Unknown," Samuel Crossman's hymn, the line that goes "Love to the loveless shown that they might lovely be."

Little is known about Samuel Crossman save that he was a seventeenth-century Anglican divine with a bachelor of divinity degree from Cambridge, who wrote nine "sacred poems" (as hymns were known in those days), and is buried in a grave on the south aisle of the Cathedral Church in Bristol. The themes of three of those other hymns do not commend him as one to whom we would turn today for spiritual uplift and guidance: "My Life's a Shade," "Earth's but a Sorry Tent," and "Farewell, Poor World, I Must Be Gone." After such advance billing one gets the feeling that already established inhabitants of that south aisle in the Cathedral Church in Bristol must have been eagerly awaiting his demise.

But "My Song Is Love Unknown" more than compensates. So let's unpack that one line and four powerful claims within it.

I

The first of these is simply the claim of *love*. We bandy that word around a great deal in our worship, and preachers are frequently prone to preach about it, often sentimentally. It is also a byword in our culture ("Make love not war") and Hollywood is frequently prone to display it, often crudely.

Crossman, needless to say, brings a special meaning to the word in the line we are considering, and has already tipped his hand by saying that he is writing about "my Savior's love," Jesus' love, God's love. There *is* a special meaning to "love" in the Christian vocabulary, and we can be reminded of it by noting how Crossman goes on to describe it. So, end of point one, one of the distinctive and much-abused Christian words is love. This is a point that cries out for elaboration.

II

So, God's love. What about it? Crossman describes it as "love to the loveless *shown*," and we need to stay with the verb for a while. How do we discover that God's love is "love to the loveless"? Because Crossman does not write "love to the loveless talked about," or even "love to the loveless preached." No, it is "love to the loveless *shown*." Love demonstrated. Love acted out. When we want to know the special character of God's love, we do not turn first to a dictionary or a theological treatise, or channel hop on TV, hoping that an evangelist will set us straight. No, if we want to learn about God's love, we look at a *deed*. We turn to the places where something is happening, where something is (in Crossman's word) being "shown."

There are many places where God's love is shown: in the wonder of this created world, which we believe is the product of love rather than chance or malevolence; in the wonder of human relationships, when we discover not only that we love somebody else but also that that somebody else loves us! In Christian terms the place where we claim to see love most clearly shown is in Jesus of Nazareth, who does not give us mere information about God's love, but acts it out, shows it to us. What Jesus *says* is important, but what Jesus *does* is even more important, and furnishes us with our best clue to what God is doing, which is loving us even when we are not aware of it, even when the evidence seems to go against it, even when we might prefer that God and love kept their distance from us, because the complications in our lives might multiply rapidly if we had to let love in the front, or even the back, door.

So rather than being an idea or a notion, love is an enactment, something *shown*.

III

That's still not enough. If love is truly shown, we still have to ask to whom it is shown, and Crossman replies that it is "love to the *loveless* shown."

There is a special meaning to the word "love" suggested by that phrase, a clue to the scripture reading as well, which necessitates a short but important detour. If I were giving a lecture right now instead of a sermon, and had a blackboard behind me instead of a chancel, I would write three words on the blackboard, and if I really wanted to impress my hearers I would write them in Greek—three different Greek words that are all translated into English by the same word, "love." (This has been a fertile source of confusion for centuries.)

The first Greek word is *philia*, meaning "brotherly or sisterly love," human affection between people, friendship. Our word "Philadelphia" is simply a transliteration of the Greek words *philia* (friendship-love) and *adelphos* (brother). Philadelphia is the place where, according to its name, brotherly (and sisterly) love should flourish, though from all reports its inhabitants have a tough time going about it. So *philia* is one kind of love: human affection, in which we share our hopes and concerns with each other.

The second Greek word is *eros*, and we are on more familiar territory with it, for our words "erotic" and "eroticism" come from it. *Eros* is love for the desirable, love for the lovable, love of the beautiful, sexual love that longs for completion in relation to the one beloved. It describes love between a man and a woman, or between two women or two men—in every case, two who are drawn together because each desires the other, and mutuality and sharing become the order of the day.

The third Greek word is *agapē*. We find few references to *philia* or *eros* in a Greek New Testament, but we find *agapē* spilling out over the top of every page. Our scripture reading is one clear example: for love, see *agapē*. In the Greek culture, dominant at the time the New Testament was written, *agapē* was a little-used and rather colorless word, pretty much wrapped up in linguistic mothballs and put on a high shelf. When the early Christians needed a special word to describe the nature of *God's* love, and neither *philia* nor *eros* would fill the bill, they took the almost unknown word *agapē*, adopted it, and redefined it to their own purposes, giving it a distinctive meaning that pointed not just to human love but particularly to divine love.

What is distinctive about *agapē*? Whereas *philia* is love to friends, and *eros* is love to the lovely, *agapē* is (in Crossman's phrase) "love to the loveless,": love toward those who don't really deserve it but are given it anyhow, whether it is returned or not; love toward those who may not realize that they are already the beneficiaries of God's love; love that takes the initiative. Paul saw this kind of love shown most distinctively (as we have previously noted) not so much in what Jesus says as in what he does. Jesus consistently reaches out in love toward all people, and people just about as consistently repudiate his love and scorn it. Their response to God's love shown to them is not to love in return, but to kill in return. Whatever else the cross may mean, it means at least that; that even when love is crucified, the crucified one keeps on loving, refusing to return spite for spite. When they pound nails into his flesh and leave him to die, his response is, "Forgive them, for they don't know what they are doing." That is the way God deals with our spite, our hatred, our rejection—simply by continuing to love us against all odds. That is *agapē*.

Don't ever call Christian love sentimental. It may appear unrealistic, or foolhardy, or too demeaning, or too costly, but sentimental it is not. It is, quite literally, hard as nails.

IV

We can handle that up to a point. "Love to the loveless shown"—a great concept, an inspiring message, a marvelous drama. But neither Crossman nor the Johannine writer end yet. There is a final part of Crossman's phrase. *Why* is "love to the loveless shown"? The answer (once again hard as nails) goes, "*that they might lovely be.*" The purpose of God's love is for the loveless to become lovely, so that they will no longer refuse God's love but accept it, embody it, and pass it on to others.

We are the "loveless," the unworthy, the undeserving, to whom God's love is offered, not just those other folks out there. Too harsh an estimate? Consider: simply on a human level, when we are loved we do not feel worthy of that love ("What can she possibly see in *me*?" or, farther down the line, "How can I ever hope to be worthy of her love?") And the answer, of course, is that I *can't* be "worthy" of her love, but the love continues to be offered anyhow. We are transformed from the loveless to those who are loved anyhow, and who can thereby begin to love in return.

If we, who do not deserve it, are loved anyhow, then we can become channels of that love to others. The message goes, "Love to the loveless shown that they [and we] might lovely be." On the level of *philia* we have human affection for a circle of friends, and that can become an ever-widening circle; on the level of *eros* we have profound sharing within a marriage bond or deep partnership, that can forever become deeper and more profound; and on the level of *agapē* we can be instruments of God's love in ways that have no boundaries whatever: toward all, toward those who threaten us, toward the folks in the office we cordially dislike, toward those whom our leaders denominate as "enemies," toward those whom the rest of the world wants to sweep under the rug and forget. That's hard work, and the only way we'll even begin to approach it is to remember again and again and again that we are already the objects of God's love.

The tune to which "My Song Is Love Unknown" is usually sung is Rhosymedre. It is not a particularly distinguished piece of music. But Ralph Vaughan Williams took that melody and surrounded it with elaborate and wonderful dissonance and countermelodies that make it quietly dazzling. It is the same with us. Just as Vaughan Williams took a relatively drab melody and made it beautiful, so God's love can transform us from ordinary drab folk to those through whom God's love can be given to others.

O God, we thank you that your love comes first, so that we don't have to create a world, but have a world in which we can respond to your love. Keep us from being placid or uncaring as beneficiaries of your love. Help us to keep rejoicing that you thought us important enough to share your life with us, in order to give us fresh ways to share that gift from you, so that it can also become a gift to others. In Jesus' name we pray. Amen.

Liberation: Cliché
or Rediscovery?

Reading: 2 Peter 3:8–13

The lectionary readings offer us a surfeit of riches: the declaration of liberation in Isaiah 40 by the prophet of the exile, who announces that a new day has dawned, even though the people are still in captivity; the anticipation of liberation that comes from the writer of Psalm 85, who relates it to justice and peace; and the writer of 2 Peter, who shores up the people's hope when liberation seems to have been too long deferred.

> Comfort my people, bring comfort to them,
> Says your God;
> Speak kindly to Jerusalem
> And promise to her
> That her term of bondage is served,
> Her penalty is paid.
>
> (Isaiah 40:1–2)

God proclaims peace to God's people and loyal servants: let them not go back to foolish ways.

Deliverance is near to those who worship God, so that glory may dwell in our land.

Love and faithfulness have come together; justice and peace have embraced.

Faithfulness appears from earth, and justice looks down from heaven. (Psalm 85:8–11)

Here is something, dear friends, which you must not forget: in God's sight one day is like a thousand years and a thousand years like one day. It is not that God is slow in keeping the divine promises, as some suppose, but that God is patient with you. It is not God's will that any should be lost, but that all should come to repentance. Since the whole universe is to dissolve, think what sort of people you ought to be, what devout and dedicated lives you should live! *Look forward to the coming of the day of the Lord, and work to hasten it on.* Relying on God's promise we look forward to new heavens and a new earth, in which justice will be established. (2 Peter 3:8–15a, italics added.)

Those who move around in certain theological circles are aware that a big word these days is "liberation," borne out of the struggle of third world Christians to escape from bondage, and coming to focus in the development of liberation theology.

If you do not move around in theological circles, the information you have just received may strike you as the biggest nonissue of our time, no more than the surfacing of a new theological cliché that will in turn be eclipsed by the next novelty on the theological scene.

In the face of that, I propose that the emphasis on liberation is not only not a cliché, but the recovery of a central part of the Christian gospel, and that far from being an exclusive concern of third world peoples, it is a message directed to those of us in the first world as well. So let us explore three claims of Christian liberation as they are emerging on the current scene, and see how they speak to us.

I

There is first of all the claim that *we are liberated from our personal sin and guilt.* This has always been a central part of the Christian message and the Jewish message out of which it springs. It is the word that goes to those exiles long ago in Babylonia, when an unknown prophet speaks the wonderful words, "Comfort my people, bring comfort to them," says God. "Speak kindly to Jerusalem and promise to her that her term of bondage is served, her penalty is paid." When we hear Handel's *Messiah,* we hear the key words as "her warfare is accomplished," but the Revised English Bible puts it even more poignantly, "her term of bondage is served." In other words, the time of liberation has come. Past debts are paid. There is a new beginning. The exiles are liberated from sin.

Now sin is not exactly a popular word on the human scene, with its implication that we are evil, repugnant, and powerless. As the old saw goes, "Being a Presbyterian may not keep me from sinning, but it sure keeps me from enjoying it." In this perspective, sin comes to mean that whatever we enjoy doing is wrong, and we are invited to fulfill H. L. Mencken's definition of Puritanism: "the awful fear that somewhere, somehow, someone might be happy."

Nor is sin the substance of the Christian message; it is only the backdrop in front of which the drama of liberation is acted out. A man comes to Jesus, recognizes in him the presence of the divine, and asks not for riches or glory or a beautiful wife or a foolproof retirement policy—he asks only to be forgiven. For the God who comes to us in Jesus of Nazareth comes with the promise that there can be a new beginning, which, I suggest, is what the venerable phrase "the forgiveness of sins" really means: a new beginning. Jesus comes with the promise that the slate has been wiped clean, that the evil past is over and done with, and that the same God he represents for us also empowers us to forgive one another, so that we can liberate one another from the power of sin over our lives.

There are none of us who do not need to hear the liberating message of the forgiveness of sins, the promise of new beginnings. There are none of us who do not yearn to put behind us whatever has been standing between us and God, or between us and other people.

Suppose we really took seriously that that is possible. Suppose we really believed that when we enter church on Sunday morning, burdened by whatever are the heavy loads of the past week, we could kneel and confess and truly believe that a fresh start had been given us, that we could begin all over again. What a fantastic liberation that would be!

Now I know it's more complicated than that—if we withhold forgiveness from another, we cannot expect to be forgiven ourselves, and we must do whatever we can to right the wrongs that made our plea for forgiveness necessary. But the bottom line is very simple: in the imagery of the passage from Isaiah, the God who speaks "kindly to Jerusalem" also speaks kindly to *us* and gives *us* comfort (which I remind you means "strength"), so that the message is, "Be strong! Be empowered!" since the terms of *our* bondage have likewise been served. All that bondage is over. We are in a brand-new situation.

II

There is a second liberation claim in Christian faith: *we can be liberated from evil structures that threaten to destroy us.* For our friends in the third world, it is the daily presence of evil structures that makes their lives so full of bondage. As a matter of sheer survival, they have learned how to identify many of them: the dictatorial regimes that stifle liberty and practice torture; ongoing civil wars in which the cream of their youth is destroyed; economic structures that handsomely reward the rich with yet more, and take from the poor even the little that they have; social mores that turn women into property; corrupt regimes that are often lavishly funded by our CIA or State Department.

That is probably not our private list of public enemies, and so the script for this part of the sermon has to be written by each of us. What are the structures in *our* lives from which we long for liberation? Is it a workplace where as early as tomorrow we may find ourselves "terminated"? Is it a crumbling marriage for which there seems to be no healing remedy? Is it an addiction to drugs or alcohol or sex or money or TV or whatever that can barely be kept under control and might erupt at any moment? Is it a sense of futility that we cannot do with our lives what we would like, since whenever we run the banner of social justice up the flagpole nobody in the congregation salutes?

We are all surrounded by structures from which we desperately need liberation. The Bible may not tell us just how to change them, but it does provide criteria by which we can judge those structures as wanting, and it also provides building blocks for new structures that must begin to take their place. There are words from Psalm 85 that initially may sound bland ("Deliverance is near to those who worship God"), but then become quite specific: "Love and faithfulness have come together; justice and peace have embraced" (which better become the lodestone for a new foreign policy almost anytime we care to look).

We must begin to look at our workplaces, our homes, our political parties, our addictive society, our churches, to see to what degree "justice and peace have embraced" or have not. Those are the criteria from all over the Bible that point us in the directions we must move if we are to be liberated from the structures of injustice that are always so perilously close to destroying us.

III

The third liberation claim is that *we can be liberated from fate,* from a sense that there is nothing we can do about anything; that events are going to unfold according to scripts utterly other than our own; that the deck is stacked; that we cannot take significant control over our own lives. Discouraged Christians frequently come to the conclusion that God wills whatever comes to pass and the most we can do is accept God's will and hope for a better deal in the next world than we have gotten in this one.

In the face of such talk, think back to the situation when Second Peter was written. This is the last book of the New Testament canon in time of composition, maybe as late as A.D. 150, which means that the only thing we know for sure about its author is that he or she could not have been the apostle Peter. The Christians the author is addressing are in a real bind. For a century they have been waiting for the return of Jesus, a return they anticipated would be surrounded with all sorts of fiery and thundering apocalyptic events. (I've omitted some of the more lurid details in the text at the beginning of this chapter, but believe me, it's fire and brimstone all the way.) Jesus, however, has not returned on the clouds of heaven, or in any other way as far as they can tell, to set up his glorious reign on earth, when the good will be rewarded and the evil punished. Now that's a hard scenario to maintain unfulfilled for a hundred years, especially when the expectation has always been that the second coming might occur, say, next Tuesday morning during the coffee break. And it is this situation of perplexity and powerlessness that the author of the letter is addressing.

And he has some encouraging things to say. Remember, he says, that God's timetable is different from yours—a thousand years to you are as a day to God, and vice versa. *Why* is it taking so long for God to fulfill the divine scenario? The author has a comforting answer: God is very patient. God wants to give plenty of time for people to hear the word. "It is not God's will," the writer affirms, "that any should be lost, but that all should come to repentance."

What will be the nature of the promised coming? "Relying on God's promise we look forward to new heavens and a new earth, in which justice will be established." So the prospect, surrounded by much furious apocalyptic imagery, is a hopeful one.

How easy it would have been for the writer to say, "Look forward to the fact that God's going to do it, not you, so just hang in there and wait—preferably in an attitude of prayer and maybe even fasting."

But no! That is *not* the message. The message is, "Look forward to the coming of the day of the Lord ["Yes, yes of course"] *and work to hasten it on* ["What?!"] This is a brand-new script. We are not to sit this one out. We are not to throw in the towel. We are not to decide there is nothing we can do. We are not to give in to fate. We *are* to see ourselves enlisted into service and activity. The day of the Lord (as both Second Peter and the psalmist and the whole Bible claim) is modeled on justice—so live justly, right now.

The message in whatever era is the same: you know from the nature of the first coming what the second coming will be. It will still involve the establishment of a realm of justice. It will be a place where, as the psalmist puts it, "justice and peace have embraced." So, writes the author, you can get to work on that right now. You don't have to wait for a divine arrival, whether in a feeding trough in a stable or on the clouds of heaven. The script for the future has *not* been carved in stone ahead of time. You can help to write it. You are not powerless in the hands of fate.

Elie Wiesel tells of a rabbinic student who complained about the way God had made the world. "You know how to make a better world?" his teacher quizzes him. "Why yes, I think I do," responds the student. "Well, then," remarks the rabbi, "get to work. There is no time to spare!"

That rabbi and the author of Second Peter have at least a few things in common.

IV

Three levels of liberation: liberation from personal sin and guilt, liberation from evil structures, and liberation from fate or a sense of powerlessness. And the most important thing about them is that *they cannot be separated*. They are not a chronological sequence, first one and then the other; they are a simultaneous challenge. We cannot decide to go for justice and ignore sin, or nudge the structures fatalistically. It is the nature of Christian liberation that it comprises all three claims, so understood that they are not finally three different things, but only three different ways of talking about the same thing.

There is a marvelous South African freedom song that goes "Freedom, O freedom, O freedom is coming, O yes I know." And we know that for South Africans the triple freedom *is* a single thing: liberation or freedom from the sin and guilt that have hampered them, liberation from the evil structure of apartheid and economic discrimination that have negated their future, and liberation from fate, which means empowerment to take things into their own hands. "Freedom, O freedom, O freedom is coming, O yes I know."

But there is a second verse as well: "Jesus, O Jesus, O Jesus is coming, O yes I know." The coming of liberation and the coming of Jesus are not two different things. They are two ways of singing about the same thing. And for us as well, the theme *is* that Jesus is coming and that freedom is coming too.

> Come, Thou long-expected Jesus,
> Born to set Thy people *free*;
> From our fears and sins release us;
> Let us find our rest in Thee.

Amen.

Reversals, Reversals, Reversals

Reading: Isaiah 61:1–4
Text: Good tidings to the afflicted . . . comfort to all who mourn . . .
that they may be called oaks of righteousness.—Isaiah 61:1, 2, 3

The first verses of the lectionary reading may sound familiar, since they are words that Jesus appropriates almost verbatim, in Luke's Gospel, to describe his Messianic agenda. So listen especially to the earlier, less familiar verses, which describe *the kinds of reversals* God has in store for anyone who will lend an ear. The passage was originally written around the fifth century B.C., which was a time of great difficulty and great opportunity for Israel—a time, in other words, much like our own.

> The Spirit of the Lord God is upon me,
> because God has anointed me
> to bring good tidings to the afflicted.
> God has sent me to bind up the brokenhearted,
> to proclaim liberty to the captives,
> and the opening of the prison to those who are bound;
> to proclaim the year of God's favor
> [and the day of rescue of our God];
> to comfort all who mourn;
> [to give them] a garland instead of ashes,
> the oil of gladness instead of mourning,
> the mantle of praise instead of a faint spirit;
> that they may be called oaks of righteousness,
> the planting of the Lord, that God may be glorified.
> [The oaks of righteousness] shall build up the ancient ruins,
> they shall raise up the former devastations;
> they shall repair the ruined cities,
> the devastations of many generations.
>
> (Isaiah 61:1–4)

Whatever our age is finally remembered for in the history books, it will be called, among other things, "a time of reversals." Things are moving along in relatively predictable patterns, and then suddenly everything gets turned around. The Berlin Wall, firmly in place for forty years, is unexpectedly assaulted and demolished without shedding of blood or loss of life. Poland is freed from political domination in a nonviolent action. Lithuania and the other Baltic states declare their independence. The apparently invincible Union of Soviet Socialist Republics crumbles beyond repair. Breaches appear in the wall of apartheid in South Africa and blacks get the right to vote. The San Francisco Giants lose seven out of ten and then win eight in a row.

We see the same pattern of reversals replicated in our individual lives. You have fallen in love—or a significant relationship has been threatened. You've been given a raise—or laid off with only a week's notice. Your child is having drug problems—or has gotten free of drug dependency. You are being transferred to Toledo—just after making the down payment on a condo. Reversals are the order of the day.

The Bible is also full of talk about reversals, sometimes called conversions, turnings about, new beginnings. And the Bible doesn't deal only with reversals worthy of mention on the six o'clock news. It also deals with interior reversals in our own lives that we dare to share only with trusted friends, and then only in a whisper. That all reversals are important is indicated by the fact that neither Isaiah nor Jesus introduces the theme by saying, "Here are some things I've been thinking about." Both of them begin by saying, "The Spirit of the Lord God is upon me, because God has anointed me to bring good tidings," after which reversals take center stage.

Let us look at Isaiah's Spirit-motivated report, in which he gives three clear examples of reversals—which suggests that somewhere along the way he must have taken a course entitled "Homiletics 101: The Art of Sermon Construction."

I

The first reversal that the passage promises is to "*the afflicted*," and we can tell from the nature of the promised reversals who the afflicted are. They are the victims, those on the bottom of the heap. Life has dealt them a series of raw deals, and they conclude that more are on the way. And no matter how well things have gone for us, there are moments when we feel ourselves among the afflicted, so Isaiah's message is for us as well.

And what is the reversal? The reversal is that those who have been conditioned to expect bad news to continue are now, perhaps for the first time, promised good news. Things are going to change. Isaiah backs up his claim with examples. The "brokenhearted," instead of being further pummeled by life, will have their wounds bound up; they will be healed. The "captives" (next on Isaiah's list), instead of being still more tightly constricted, will be liberated. And just in case there's any doubt about how real the reversals are going to be, Isaiah tells us that the "prisoners" (even those named Nelson Mandela), instead of being denied parole, or having their sentences further extended, will discover that the prison doors are open, and they are free.

Now that is a happy agenda, full of promises and gifts that none of the afflicted would have anticipated or counted on. But we won't have done full justice to the text until we consider the *overall reversal* to which Isaiah points: he must also "proclaim the year of God's favor." The translators were a little chicken when it came to that verse, for the apparently innocuous phrase about "the year of God's favor" was actually a specific, not at all innocuous vision of what Isaiah proclaimed—what the book of Leviticus had called "a jubilee year." This was to take place every fifty years, and it had some exhilarating and alarming characteristics: (1) *All debts would be canceled.* You're in over your head to a loan shark or a pawnbroker? They won't come and foreclose on you; the debt will be wiped out. (2) *All slaves would be freed.* You're in hock up to your elbows and the person over you is calling all the shots for your life? That's going to come to an end. (3, and hold our breath on this one) *Capital would be redistributed.* Leviticus reports that the people who have been racking it up by foreclosing on the poor, the perpetrators of unfriendly takeovers or union-busting tactics, not to mention the ones who have made millions and don't care what happens to anyone else—all these with ill-gotten gains will find those gains being redistributed so that the ordinary folks can start all over again and look ahead with hope.

The people in charge didn't exactly enthuse over that agenda, and as far as we know, the vision of a jubilee year never actually got off the ground. But it has remained ever since as *a symbol of hope*—a centrally biblical hope—a declaration that things don't have to stay the way they are. There can be change, not just for the worse but for the better, and the victims, the poor, the afflicted (whoever they may be) are the targets of this message. *Things can be reversed.* Whether that's good news or bad news depends on whether we are on the top or the bottom of the heap.

II

Isaiah doesn't just deal with what might be called a broad social message. The promise of reversals is extended to a second group of people, "*all who mourn,*" those for whom joy has become alien, whose inner lives, if not their outer circumstances, have been terribly scarred, for whom the bottom seems to have dropped out of things: the death of a loved one, anxiety about the workplace, the fear of cancer, the loss of self-esteem, the emptiness that comes when hopes and dreams have been shattered.

The basic reversal promised here is a movement from *mourning to comfort*. We need to recall again what we discovered about that word "comfort." Too often it sounds like a little verbal pat on the back after something terrible has happened, with neutral words ("There . . . there . . . ") sometimes followed by demonic words ("I'm sure it's all for the best") precisely at the moment when you know it's *not* all for the best. Rather than such syrupy consolation, Isaiah offers comfort. The word comes from the Latin *com-fortis,* and it means "with strength," strong as a fortress. The giving of comfort, therefore, is the sharing of strength, the sharing of oneself, the offer of help and assistance, the assurance, "You're not alone in this; there are others who will be with you, who will share the burden, so don't throw in the towel. Help is here, and more is on the way."

Example: Recently a college roommate spent an evening with Sydney and me. He had been best man at our wedding. And four months ago his wife, partner in a forty-five year marriage had died, only shortly after a diagnosis of cancer. He was shattered; but also, unexpectedly, strengthened, and commenting on the way friends had rallied around him, he said, "All this terrible grief and anger and pain—and yet in the midst of it so . . . much . . . love."

Notice how, in images from his own day, Isaiah insists and insists and insists on reversals, new beginnings, for those who mourn. Instead of "ashes" (symbols of defeat or destruction), you'll get a "garland" (the prize that in the ancient world was given to those who won an athletic contest, analogous to getting a gold medal in the Olympics today). "Mourning," he goes on, will be replaced by the "oil of gladness" (a reversal easily understood in a culture where the act of anointing with oil was an indication of God's favor). So if having your head anointed with oil sounds like a messy project at best, remember that in Isaiah's time it was a clear metaphor for moving from mourning to joy.

There is another reversal for "those who mourn." Instead of what Isaiah calls "a faint spirit," an expression of fear and timidity and powerlessness, there will be "a mantle of praise," an accolade for those who have given it everything they've got. In our culture the image might be a twenty-one gun salute, or receiving the Most Valuable Player award, or, if your initials are W. J. C., having the band play "Hail to the Chief" at almost any public occasion where you are present. Those who mourn will be affirmed rather than shunned.

III

There is a third way in which Isaiah describes reversals, and it is essential to emphasize it if we are to understand the first two reversals so that they aren't reduced to whistling in the dark or making Pollyanna-like noises that everything is really just peachy.

Those who experience reversals will become, in Isaiah's words, *"oaks of righteousness,"* planted by God. That's a splendid image. Oaks are noted for being durable and large and strong, in contrast to weak reeds or tiny trees that can't survive heavy winds or bad weather. In the earlier reversals (for the afflicted and those who mourn) the gift of new beginnings is given without any strings attached. But when God promises to make us "oaks of righteousness," a task is imposed. If we are truly to be "oaks of righteousness," we are to bestir ourselves, and participate directly in creating new conditions for others. *We are to be the instruments through whom God brings about the reversals.* This text doesn't just give us a promise, it gives us a series of marching orders. Listen to the agenda that is laid on the "oaks of righteousness":

> They shall build up the ancient ruins; they shall raise up
> the former devastations; they shall repair the ruined cities,
> the devastation of many generations.

If there is a ruling *image* here, it is "devastations"—the realization that things are in bad shape. No one can look at our broken world today and deny that Isaiah's descriptions still apply: the devastation of the homeless, the devastation of drug victims, the devastation of victims of death squads, the devastation of those who know they are about to lose their jobs, the devastation of families who can no longer hear one another. The ruling image is a strong image of devastation.

But the ruling *imperative* is equally strong. Look at the verbs Isaiah marshals: "build up . . . raise up . . . repair." Those are verbs that are meant to describe us. We are not to sit back and wait for God to do all that. We are to be the ones *through whom* God does all that. To the degree that God has effected reversals in our lives, we must work to effect reversals in other people's lives. And if we are still looking for some of those reversals for our own lives, and feel that God has been pretty stingy in dealing them out to us, we are nevertheless to get on with helping to create reversals in *other* lives—and making the extraordinary discovery (one of the real surprises of the gospel) that as we do so, reversals will begin to come unbidden and unsought into our own lives as well.

There are no limits to the ways we can be "oaks of righteousness": keeping a one-on-one relationship where cancer has struck; politicking for maternity and paternity leave in the workplace; sharing the personal insecurity of another; working to stop the resumption of military aid to nations under the grip of dictators.

Those situations and hundreds of others like them are instances of the "devastations" that Isaiah indicates we are not to accept passively but to fight actively. We are "to build up, to raise up, to repair, . . . to effect reversals."

O God, father and mother of us all, you wish only good for us despite our evil. We thank you that the last word has not been written on our lives, and that there is no situation in which it is impossible to start moving in new directions. We know we can't do this on our own, but we also know that if you empower us, we can be instruments for fulfilling your intentions for the entire human family in whose midst you have placed us. And for this we say, thanks be to you; through Jesus Christ our Lord. Amen.

Reconciliation:
The Bottom Line

Reading: 2 Corinthians 5:17–20
Text: God was in Christ reconciling the world to God . . . and has entrusted us with the message of reconciliation.—2 Corinthians 5:19

A twelve-volume commentary, *The Interpreter's Bible,* refers to 2 Corinthians
5:11–20 as "the heart of the gospel. No passage in [Paul's] letters is more
important." When the Presbyterian Church adopted the Confession of 1967,
it was organized around the same words: the writers of the confession declared that there was no other passage that more fully encapsulated the
Christian message.

The words were written by Paul to the obstreperous church at Corinth. He
was writing out of his own experience as a strong persecutor of the early Christians before his sudden conversion on the road to Damascus. If anyone had
stood in need of being "reconciled" with God it was Paul, and we can read this
classic statement of faith as Paul's personal confession of what surely was for
him the bottom line.

> For anyone united to Christ there is a new creation; the old order has gone;
> a new order has already begun.
> All this has been the work of God. God has reconciled us to God through
> Christ, and has enlisted us in the ministry of reconciliation. In Christ God was
> reconciling the world to God, no longer holding people's misdeeds against
> them, and has entrusted us with the message of reconciliation. We are there-
> fore Christ's ambassadors. It is as if God were appealing to you through us;
> we implore you in Christ's name, be reconciled to God. (2 Corinthians 5:17–20)

We are all familiar with the phrase "the bottom line," that which, no matter what happens, we refuse to compromise or discard. For some people it
is the sanctity of life ("Whatever happens I could never kill another human being"). For others, it is the sanctity of truth ("I could never tell a lie").

A soldier might decide, "I will kill if necessary but I will never inflict torture, even to save my life." Albert Camus has a play about a revolutionary who is all set to throw a bomb into the emperor's carriage, but when the carriage passes by, he cannot throw the bomb. Why not? Because the emperor's children were in the carriage and he could not bring himself to murder children. He, too, had a bottom line.

There is a bottom line for Christians concerning how much of their faith they are willing to surrender as nonessential, and how much they will at all costs refuse to negotiate away. Different Christians draw the line at different places. One may say, "I draw the line at scripture. I refuse to give up anything that's in the Bible." Another might say, "I'd be willing to put some items of my faith up for grabs, like the difference between infralapsarians and supralapsarians. But there is at least one item that isn't negotiable, and that is the claim that the person of Jesus Christ makes a decisive difference in our relationship to God. Everything else could go, but not that. The heart of the gospel is that Christ reconciles us to God. Take that away and there's nothing left. It's the bottom line."

So let's examine it.

I

The first thing we discover is that whatever this reconciliation business is all about (and we'll come to that shortly), *it is not just a promise for the future but a claim about the present.*

This is not what we would have expected. If somebody purports to offer us a brand-new situation, we are usually realistic enough (and cynical enough) not to pretend that it has already arrived. Presidential campaigns are built on no more, and no less, than this premise. "Change"—something new—is what every candidate is selling. Things aren't great now, they acknowledge, but look ahead! By the simple act of casting your vote for X rather than Y you can ensure change. The future can be better than the past. Forget about the present, which is hardly good news to anyone. Good news belongs to the future tense.

But not when Paul is talking. We would expect Paul to start out with a timetable similar to that employed by candidates for public office something like: "Listen, friends, for anyone united in Christ there is going to be a brand-new creation; the old order is going to disappear; a new order will come pretty soon. Look to the future, folks, salvation is just around the corner."

But Paul doesn't say it that way at all. Flying in the face of substantial evidence to the contrary, *he announces good news in the present tense.* "For anyone united in Christ there *is* a new creation. The old order has gone. A new order has *already* been born." He is writing about a present reality, something in the here and now, better news than we have ever heard before.

And it all sounds preposterous! We are part of a "new creation" *now*? We live in a world where "the old order has gone away"?—a world in which "a new order has already begun"? Not very convincing, Brother Paul. Your enthusiasm has gotten the better of you. Let's get realistic about our world: Camelot it's not. Our world is a world of war and the constant threat of war, homelessness, the capricious spread of cancer, senseless automobile accidents, surgery gone awry, rampant unemployment. We know the litany of woes. So our incredulous question, as we look around us, remains: *This* is the "new creation"?

For whatever consolation it provides, this is an instance of the perennial Christian dilemma: there is no way we can escape the claim of Jesus and Paul that this is a new situation, but there is also no way we can escape the fact that the old situation is holding on fast and refusing to surrender any significant territory.

The choice we face goes something like this: either we insist that the old situation is the only reality there is, that the glimpses and glimmers we get of something better are too fragile to be taken seriously, so that we must make our peace in whatever way we can; or we throw in our lot with the glimpses and glimmers of something new and bet our lives on the possibility that they represent a radical new direction that is available right now.

It is already a brand-new situation and we can take part in it if we choose to.

II

How do we "choose to"? How do we become part of this new reality about which Paul writes so enthusiastically? His answer is unequivocal: there is nothing we can do to change the situation, *for God has already done whatever needs to be done.* It is all God's work. It is God who takes the initiative, God who crosses over the distance that separates us, (or, to use Paul's terminology), God who does the reconciling.

"God who does the reconciling . . . " Whatever does that mean?

Let us approach it through the back door. The most accurate word, surely, to describe the opposite of "reconciliation" is "estrangement," or "separation." And even though we may not be very clear about what reconciliation is, we are very clear indeed about what estrangement is, for we have all experienced it. You don't have to be a French existentialist or a devotee of Søren Kierkegaard to realize that we live daily in the midst of estrangement. One of Albert Camus's early novels was called *L'Étranger,* usually translated "the stranger," but by some scholars as "the outsider." And we are both. To be estranged is to be a stranger, one without close connections, and to be an outsider is to feel neglected, overlooked, or even actively excluded. To be estranged, then, is to be separated, cut off, lacking connections. When we take the word in its fullest meaning, we discover that we are estranged (a) from one another, (b) from creation, the world in which we live, and (c) from God—all three in varying and changing proportions. Estrangement? Welcome to the club.

And the overcoming of estrangement is reconciliation—no longer being separated from one another, but united once again; no longer cut off from one another, but in communication; no longer strangers to one another, but friends and lovers who can share fully; no longer at loose ends, but standing on firm ground. Reconciliation is most profoundly the restoring of personal relationships with other human beings, with creation, and with God.

It is Paul's extravagant claim that that is exactly what has happened in God's gift to us of Jesus Christ: the breach between God and ourselves and our world has been overcome. Distance has been replaced by closeness. There is no way we can make our way to God, but God has rendered that unnecessary by making a way to us, embodied in the human life of Jesus of Nazareth, who shared our lot totally. Not only that, Paul declares on every page, but when we did our worst to Jesus, not even that could negate God's reconciling love, for death was followed by resurrection. Not even death has the final say anymore. However we deal with that colossal claim about a resurrection, it means, if true, that the new order *is* already here, and that it is the work of God. And that reality of reconciliation, more powerful than estrangement, can enter every corner of our lives.

We all have moments when estrangement seems to have won the day—human relationships spoiled, our relation to creation exploitive, the reality of God depressingly, if not menacingly, absent. How, then, can we still take reconciliation seriously? Only, I think, by searching our hearts to recall moments, however few, when we knew not only what estrangement *was* but also what reconciliation *is*—after a spat with a spouse, or friend or lover, when deep love has been restored; after a misunderstanding on the playground when two angry children have put it behind them (kids are very good at reconciliation); after a shattering disappointment, when somebody helped us begin to put the pieces together again; after railing against God, and then discovering that estrangement was no longer the name of the game, and reconciliation was.

Once again we face a choice. This time our gigantic leap of faith is to believe that the moments when reconciliation is real are the moments closest to the way things really are, and that we are to build on them, trust in them, and let them more and more direct the course of our lives.

III

So far, it's all about God's activity, God's initiative, God's reconciling act. But that is far from the whole story. There is a third emphasis in the passage, and it deals with us. It is important enough for Paul to mention it three times in as many verses: (a) God "has enlisted us in the ministry of reconciliation," (b) God "has entrusted us with the message of reconciliation," and (c) "we are therefore Christ's ambassadors." If reconciliation seems initially one-sided, it now becomes two-sided. If we have been given the gift of reconciliation, we have to live it, we have to share it, we have to make sure the word gets around. We have to be reconcilers ourselves. We have to be, and let's use Paul's words, *ambassadors of reconciliation.*

Ambassadors are people who have been validated by their government to transact business on the government's behalf, to be message bearers to other political powers, not trying to "sell" themselves, but trying to argue persuasively for the concerns of those they represent. And it is that task to which we have been set apart, to be ambassadors of reconciliation.

Before you reply, "That lets me off the hook; I'm too unimportant to be an ambassador," let me remind you of one of the great saints of our time, Archbishop Oscar Romero, and how he was an ambassador of reconciliation in El Salvador. People sometimes respond, "Oh, but he was special, a public figure, an archbishop." But the real secret of the Romero story is that Oscar Romero was very ordinary. As a young man he didn't stand out from the crowd. He wasn't a born leader or a spellbinding orator (though he used to preach for an hour and forty-five minutes during mass!). He was picked to be archbishop of San Salvador, at a tense time in El Salvador's history, precisely because he *was* "ordinary" and could be trusted not to cause any problems to church or state by getting out of line. But God used the life and martyr's death of this ordinary "man of the people," to do great things, siding with the poor, attacking the despots, challenging the powerful. Romero's story means that we can never write our own stories on the assumption that we are too unimportant to make a difference. As Paul reminds us in his first letter to the Corinthians, "God chose the weak things of the world to confound the strong: (see 1 Cor. 1:18–24).

The business of being ambassadors of reconciliation applies very clearly in one-on-one relationships, at which we are pretty good. But the gospel always stretches us beyond where we are, for reconciliation is to inform all that we do. In the text, God was not just reconciling the disciples, or the

Jews, or the Jews and the Gentiles, or the poor and the rich, God was reconciling the *world*. The Greek word Paul uses is even stronger—*ho kosmos* (the cosmos), "planet earth," the whole of the created order, our galaxy, the universe—all that is. Nothing is beyond the range of God's reconciling activity. And the conclusion that follows is pretty clear: *if God reaches out to achieve reconciliation everywhere, so must we*. Random examples:

We are ambassadors of reconciliation when we establish creative rather than destructive relationships between nature and human nature, between the goodness of God's creation and the mess we have made of it—and that means not only new attitudes but new laws and regulations about such things as toxic dumping outside our factories.

We are ambassadors of reconciliation when we refuse to trash other persons because they are Jews or Muslims, gays or lesbians, Japanese car manufacturers or workers on a Detroit assembly line, people whose politics or theology we abhor.

We are ambassadors of reconciliation when we work to change unjust laws that discriminate against the poor or the homeless or people on welfare, or unmarried teenage mothers—all of which means an ongoing critical look at priorities within our federal and state and city budgets.

Reconciliation, then, isn't just being nice to people, or trying to avoid conflict. Indeed, reconciliation is only needed from within already existing conflict. Ambassadors of reconciliation need to be tough-minded and take sides, working precisely in the midst of estrangement, working in local politics, working for fairer tax laws, working for better health care for the poor and for everyone.

It's a stern agenda, being an ambassador of reconciliation. But the word from on high is to rejoice. Why? Because we live in a brand-new situation, because God has reconciled us to one another, and because we have the privilege of being ambassadors of that reconciling love ourselves. Those are the givens of the Christian story. Let them empower us to move in new directions, so that the story is more widely heard and more widely believed.

O God, we thank you for breaking through our estrangement with your reconciling love, to reestablish full relationship with us. We are sorry for the times we live as though that were not so, and make a lie of your truth. Show us those places where all of us are called to be ambassadors of reconciliation, and empower us to move in new and sometimes lonely directions. In the name of Jesus, whom you sent to be the agent of your reconciling love, we pray. Amen.

Part 2
Exploring a Terrain

We do not communicate only with words and formal concepts. We actually communicate much better with stories, and the church has provided a handy framework within which to do this. It is called the Christian year, and it is a retelling of the Jesus story as a year-long drama. It begins with anticipation of Jesus' coming (Advent), and moves through his birth and "manifestation" to the world (Epiphany), on to events within his ministry (including the transfiguration), into the climactic events leading to his death (Palm Sunday and Good Friday), his resurrection (Easter), and reflection on the meaning of his coming (Trinity Sunday and beyond). This is the pattern followed in Part 2. Most of the sermons are deliberately offbeat to enable us to see familiar material in unfamiliar ways, and recapture the story motif that is so often overlaid with ponderous prose.

– 8 –

The Official and Unofficial Reports
of a Lower Echelon Functionary
in Herod's Court (Advent)

Readings: Isaiah 2:1–5; Matthew 24:36–44
Text: Keep awake, then, for you do not know on what day your
Sovereign will come. . . . Hold yourselves ready, therefore, because
the Son of Man will come at the time you least expect him.
—Matthew 24:42, 44

The compilers of the lectionary throw us a curveball during Advent. The portions from the Hebrew Scriptures are foretelling the coming of a Messiah who has not yet appeared. The New Testament passages, on the other hand, not only presuppose a first coming but look forward to a second. As Martin Buber has pointed out, the biggest single difference between Jews and Christians is that while we are both messianic faiths, when it comes to cataloging how Messiahs come and go, we have very different timetables.

The mood in the Gospel lesson (and all the passages that surround it) is that nobody except God knows when the final clarification will take place no matter what the fundamentalists of every era try to tell us. So the recurring advice is: expect the unexpected. Stay awake. Keep watching. You never know when the big event is about to happen.

> Yet about that day and hour [of the messianic arrival] no one knows, not even the angels in heaven, not even the Son: no one but God alone knows.
>
> As it was in the days before the flood, they ate and drank and married, until the day that Noah went into the ark, and they knew nothing until the flood came and swept them all away. That is how it will be when the Son of Man comes. Then there will be two men in the field; one will be taken, the other left; two women grinding at the mill; one will be taken, the other left.
>
> Keep awake, then, for you do not know on what day your God will come. Remember, if the householder had known at what time of night the burglar was coming, he would have stayed awake and not let his house be broken into. Hold yourselves ready, therefore, because the Son of Man will come at the time you least expect him. (Matthew 22:36–44)

47

It's a fidgety time. Nothing is going well. The chariots are not running on schedule. Caesar is throwing his weight around again, this time in the person of Herod, the local procurator who takes all his orders from Rome and is executing political prisoners right and left to quell any possible uprising. He does so at virtually no cost to the taxpayers, as he is fond of pointing out, since the wooden crosses used for public executions are very durable and can be recycled for use again and again, thereby conserving the forests up north. Caesar clearly wants to be remembered as the Environmental Emperor.

The Greeks are still mumbling about a Golden Age, just over the horizon, they claim, but their hearts are not in it, and to the rest of us, talk about a Golden Age is just an intellectual game, a harmless diversion that keeps the philosophers out of the gambling halls.

The social planners have a new scheme for ordering society that they will present to the proper authorities, as soon as they have figured out how to abolish greed.

The astrologers tell us that even the heavens are acting up, and that what is apparently a conjunction of several planets is beginning to dominate the eastern sky.

So it's a fidgety time. And in addition, just to keep things complicated, there are the Jews, who keep turning up all over the empire. Just now they are recycling their stories about the immanent arrival of one whom they call a *Mashiah,* or as we would say a Messiah, an Anointed One sent from God, who will set everything to rights. It's a comforting notion even for those of us who are not Jews. Unfortunately, they've been parading this line for four hundred years without producing any results, so it's a little hard to take it seriously anymore, especially when one remembers that the Jews are at the absolute bottom of the social order—not a place one looks to for signs of hope.

However, just as with all minority groups in the empire, someone has to keep tabs on them and, for better or worse, that job has fallen unbidden into my lap for decades—ever the plight of a lower functionary in a massive bureaucracy. And so, once again, the annual report is due, and I've been taking random samplings among the Jews, trying to see if there are any new wrinkles on this Messiah business.

1. The messianic scenario I hear bruited about, though not (for obvious reasons) trumpeted in the village square, could be called *The Exterminator—Part One.* It's laid out in their book of Daniel. Some Jews argue that they have gotten such a rotten deal as the continually persecuted minority that the only way God can really make it up to them is to appear as a great warrior-king (preferably on the clouds of heaven), take full charge,

drive the occupying Roman forces back into the sea, and establish God's rule on earth.

The Messiah will be called "the Son of Man," even though he is always a heavenly creature, God operating in high gear. Before the naked power of God's sword, wielded by the heavenly Messiah, all the enemies will melt away or be slain. Naturally, the worse things get for the Jews (or any oppressed people) the more such a scenario appeals.

Understandably, however, the proposal doesn't sit well with the local garrisons of Roman soldiers, many of them far from home, who are always ready to liquidate anybody who even whispers such a proposal.

2. A second less bloodthirsty scenario could be called *The Davidic Connection*. There will be a Messiah all right, no doubt about that, but he will have to possess the credential of being a descendant of King David, with ancestors going back to the time when David ruled—the greatest period in Jewish history, a history that ever since seems to have been going downhill. David's descendant will reestablish the monarchy, which will inaugurate an era of justice and peace on earth.

Sometimes there is a gentler version, championed by those who remember that before David was a monarch he was a shepherd. Many folks in the rural areas like to think of the restoration of the Davidic line as the return to a pastoral existence, ruled by one who acts like a shepherd, caring for the sheep, seeing that they don't get lost, taking them to new grazing grounds, showing the farmers how to make swords into plowshares, and so forth.

3. There's another way the messianic hopes get stirred up. We could almost call it *The Exterminator—Part Two*. The vengeful Exterminator begins to show another side than doom and bloodshed and exhibits care and identification with the people. Since it's a hard one to understand, we might also call it *Messiah: The Story behind the Man,* or if anybody is working on a doctoral dissertation, *A Case Study in Redefinition, with Special Attention to the Hopes for a* Mashiah *in Ancient Israel.*

It goes something like this: In the never-ending human power struggle, there is inevitably immense suffering. If someone hits you, survival dictates that you hit back; if someone inflicts suffering on you, survival dictates that you inflict suffering in return. According to the theory, that's the Real World. It's a heads-I-win-tails-you-lose sort of situation. And opposing all that is the strange idea that the Messiah won't come just to smash everybody's heads together, but to make himself vulnerable, by letting the blows fall on him without retaliating in kind, trying to bind up the wounds rather than multiplying them, being, as one of their later writers put it, "a suffering servant."

Now on the face of it that's not an appealing notion at all. If the one you look on as a potential deliverer turns out to be a loser, who needs him? So you'd think such a proposal would die immediately for want of a second. But it nevertheless persists. It would surely mean a brand-new vision of who God is, and what true power is, and what a God with that kind of power would do. The net result, I must confess, has a certain attractiveness, namely, that if suffering is part of the package, the notion that God is in the midst of the suffering, right here with us, has some appeal. (The appeal is tempered by the realization that people who act like that have a track record of ending up on Caesar's recyclable crosses.) If God were present not only in the good, but in the bad and the ugly as well, we'd have some reasons to stay involved in the struggle against the bad and the ugly, because God would be there too.

Anyhow, strange as it is, it's part of the evidence, and I am duty bound to include it. End of Official Report.

Now you must allow an old man to do some speculating. None of this will be included with the Official Report, and nobody will ever see it until after my death. I know better than to take on a power structure, even timidly. So I'm simply asking myself what it would be like to take this Messiah business with something more than a grain of salt. Or, to put it another way, what kind of Messiah does the world really need?

The way I figure it, he'd be a now-you-see-him-now-you-don't sort of character, popping up here and there when least expected, so you'd always have to be on the lookout. If I were to write a *Handbook on How to Recognize the Real Messiah When He Finally Comes*, I'd have to say something like this: nobody, but nobody, not even the Messiah himself, not even the angels in heaven know when he's coming. Only God knows, and God's not talking. So it means being on the ready every moment. The key mood would be anticipation, and realizing you had to keep looking everywhere all the time, never knowing what you'd find.

I'd even consider (and I scarcely dare even to write this because it is blasphemous) that the role might be played by a woman—which would certainly highlight the idea of the Messiah appearing in forms and guises we didn't expect. If I were to explore that idea in detail, Caesar would have me up on one of those crosses in a jiffy. Anyhow, that's my supersecret scenario, and where I say "him," be subversive and think "her" if it helps.

So I'd begin by scratching away the notion of the Messiah appearing exclusively among the high and mighty of this world, which, of course, is where his enemies would look for him. Come to think of it—and what a delicious irony this would be—the best place for him to show up consistently would be among the Jews themselves. Nobody would think of looking for him there. The phrase "salvation is of the Jews" has always been laughed out of court. Then I'd let him grow up in the boondocks, some such place as Nazareth, since the scornful question, "Can any good thing come out of Nazareth?" has always been answered in the negative.

Friends and acquaintances? H'mm. I think I'd have him hobnob with the dregs of society—tax collectors, prostitutes, Syrians. Profession? Not a courtier or a general or a computer analyst, but somebody with a blue-collar job—a plumber, or a garage mechanic, or even a carpenter.

What should he do as Messiah? I'd be willing to grant him some special gifts of healing. That usually goes with the territory, and it certainly couldn't do any harm. I'd make sure he stayed away from army recruitment centers, and I'd give him considerable time to be something like a rabbi or teacher. But not, for heaven's sake, a credentialed teacher! No Ph.D. for him, and surely no more than a high school equivalency diploma. So he'd teach, but the things he'd teach would be fairly obvious: love one another, don't cheat on your marriage partner, identify with the struggles of the poor and powerless, don't give the empire the kind of support that belongs only to God, liberate the folks from fear and trembling, and so on.

Actually, as far as the teaching went, the really important thing would be that he didn't just say them, but that he lived them. That would interest people at first, though it would probably frighten them at last, for if *he* lived them out, that would mean that *we* were supposed to live them out too, and that might turn out to be a direct route to a cross.

People would watch him and try to psych him out: was he for real or was he a charlatan? It might be hard to tell, because all that "simple" stuff he taught would turn out, on closer examination, to be revolutionary stuff. And things would get even more dicey when the authorities began to tail him for fear the common people might respond to him and challenge those same authorities in his name. They'd be worried enough to infiltrate his inner circle with a double agent, to get the goods on him. And they'd get the goods on him all right. There would be a smoking gun, consisting of subversive talk and action, labeled love and justice.

So they'd kill him as a subversive and that would be the end of the Messiah. Nice try, God, better luck next time.

(Of course, if I were really on a narrative roll, I'd go the whole way and invoke my powers as an author to raise him from the dead—a kind of divine "Ha! ha!" against the principalities and powers. But of course, that's beyond the realm of the credible, and we need to have a story people might believe.)

Well, after such an exercise I'd have to ask myself, What's so messianic about all this? To me, the answer is pretty clear: *This man would keep bugging me.* I'd see him teaching, and maybe be put off by what he'd said and think I'd disposed of him, and then bingo he'd be healing my sister-in-law. Or I'd dispose of him by thinking, Ah, he's a Jew, so he's not for me, and then I'd see him blessing little children—not just Jewish children, but Gentile children, Phoenician children, Syrian children, whatever. Or I'd be lashing out at some stupid corporal in the praetorian guard, and he'd just happen to walk past saying, "Love your enemies."

Now you see him now you don't. Just when you thought you had a line on him, he'd turn out to be something quite different. Every moment would be the moment just before he might appear, or disappear, or hang around for a while. And you'd never know ahead of time which it would be.

When the historians look back on our era, I wonder what they'll see. That it was another generation in which the Messiah didn't come? Or that he did come and nobody noticed? Maybe far into the future people will still be keeping watch, never knowing where he might turn up again. In the meantime I guess the way you'd prepare for a Messiah would be to try to do little messianic deeds yourself—love for the neighbor, care for the enemy, justice for the oppressed—the whole package. Then, if the Messiah came, you and he would already be on the same wavelength.

But when you get realistic, you have to conclude that it's likely a pipe dream, which is probably for the best, because if we *did* start taking it seriously, we'd have to be out there turning the world upside down. And nobody, not even God, would dream up a scenario like that.

Fortunately.

O God, we thank you that even in our most strong-willed moments, we can't quite shake off this impossible dream that our lives could be moved in new directions. So help us, once more, to entertain the vision that someone is still coming, one whom we have welcomed many times before and then forgotten. This time around help us to keep alive the dangerous memory of Jesus of Nazareth, and what could be accomplished through him, in whose name we pray. Amen.

Three Messengers
(Which Is What the Greek Word *Angelos* Means)
Discuss Past and Future Assignments
(Epiphany)

Reading: Matthew 2:1–12
Text: King Herod was greatly perturbed.—Matthew 2:3

The word "Epiphany" does not roll off our tongues with the same facility as, say, Christmas, Easter, or Good Friday. It's in a category similar to Maundy Thursday; we're not quite sure how to pronounce it, and even less sure what it means.

An epiphany is a manifestation, a showing forth—in this case the showing forth to the entire world of one to whom the story gives the title "King of the Jews." The early Christians—Jews, all of them—soon realized that celebrating the birth of the King of the Jews could not remain an event exclusively for Christians of Jewish origin, for the Messiah, or the Anointed One, was sent for all people whatever their background, not only Jewish shepherds but Gentile astrologers as well.

So Epiphany is the time we celebrate the *universality* of the Christmas message—an invitation not only to hear the story but to enter into it and make it a part of our lives. The story—better still, the legend—about the Wise Men and the camels grew gradually over many centuries; the names of the "kings," for example, do not appear in the telling until the sixth century. The sermon is a non-credentialed account of how the story might originally have come into being.

Jesus was born at Bethlehem in Judaea during the reign of Herod. After his birth astrologers from the east arrived in Jerusalem, asking, "Where is the child who is born to be king of the Jews? We observed the rising of a star, and have come to pay him homage." King Herod was greatly perturbed when he heard this; and so was the whole of Jerusalem. He called a meeting of the chief priests and lawyers of the Jewish people, and put before them the question, "Where is it that the Messiah is to be born?" "At Bethlehem in Judaea," they replied; and they referred him to the prophecy which reads: "Bethlehem in the land of Judah, you are far from least in the eyes of the rulers of Judah; for out of you shall come a leader to be the shepherd of my people Israel."

Herod next called the astrologers to meet him in private, and ascertained from them the time when the star had appeared. He then sent them on to Bethlehem, and said, "Go and make a careful inquiry for the child. When you have found him, report to me, so that I may go myself and pay him homage."

They set out at the king's bidding; and the star which they had seen at its rising went ahead of them until it stopped above the place where the child lay. At the sight of the star they were overjoyed. Entering the house, they saw the child with Mary his mother, and bowed to the ground in homage to him; then they opened their treasures and offered him gifts: gold, frankincense, and myrrh. And being warned in a dream not to go back to Herod, they returned home another way. (Matthew 2:1–12)

Okay, group, let's come to order. The Boss has given us a really tough assignment this time. The last one was tough enough, but it was doable; construct a story about the way the Boss comes to live on earth, just like the earthlings themselves, and shares their lot by becoming one of them. Michael, I must say you deserve a lot of credit for seizing on that shepherd imagery from the Written Books, as a way of disabusing people of the notion that the Boss would probably lead a military conquest from outer space. And it was sheer genius to figure out that the best way to get the message across about shepherds would be to beam it to . . . shepherds themselves.

Anyhow, that worked very well, and as sure as my name is Gabriel, the shepherds got the message and went to Bethlehem and found that it really was about a baby. After the baby grows up, of course he will show the earthlings what the Boss is really like in human form, and make clear that they are supposed to be like the Boss themselves. That idea is not so hard for the earthlings to understand; they just think it's unpleasant to be asked to put it into practice. As we know, they find a thousand reasons to turn off that l-o-v-e business the minute it begins to get costly.

Well, the word is out now in the region of Judah that the Boss has put in a highly unexpected type of appearance—and congratulations once again, Michael, for a very tidy script.

But that was last week. The real stuff as you'll see is about to begin, and it's going to take a lot of overtime to meet the Boss's schedule. The Boss wants the rest of the story, or a sequel to it, or however we want to do it, and he wants it ready for distribution within the week; says people might think the story is only a local story for the folks in Judah, whereas the truth is that the story is for everybody on the whole cockeyed planet; wants the *full* story out before any earthlings get the wrong idea.

Raphael, you pointed out quite rightly before the meeting that the Boss has been doing the *local* thing for centuries: Moses in *Egypt,* Amos in *Bethel,* Isaiah's successor in *Babylon*—always in some specific place. What they now want Upstairs is not just a message for folks in one place but in *every* place. And frankly, short of a cosmic disruption, I don't yet have the foggiest notion how we're going to pull that off in a way that doesn't stretch the earthlings' credulity too much. You know the rules: it's okay to strain credulity a bit—that's always been our job—and it helps remind the earthlings who's really in charge. But we *still* have to come up with something they won't dismiss as nonsense.

I'm the first to admit that my original notion of a cosmic disruption would shatter the universe and destroy everybody we were trying to reach—which is a considerable mark against its appropriateness in this situation. We could, of course, propose that the Boss touch down somewhere on the planet and initiate a state-of-the-art tour of everywhere else, but if so we're talking thousands of stops and starts, aided by massive tailwinds all the way. So what say we cross cosmic destruction off the list of possible scripts.

What's that, Raphael? Turn it around? What do you mean? This time instead of sending the Boss to the people, send the people to the Boss? Have the new crowd the Boss wants to reach make a trek to Bethlehem, just like the shepherds did, only this time have them come from all parts of the planet? Yes, that would be complicated, but let's feed it into the computer and see what comes out.

In the meantime, what are we talking? caravans? population shifts? census regulations? No, we used census regulations last week, just to get Mary and Joseph on the road. Anyhow, so far it sounds more like Cecil B. De Mille than the Boss, and you know how the Boss hates to be upstaged by Cecil B. De Mille and Charlton Heston.

Let's downsize it a bit and see what happens. What if we had only a few people go, representing the others? And then, when they returned, they'd have to tell the others all about it, and the others would have to tell still more others. The campaign slogan could be "Each one teach one" even though that one has been used before and—hey! I'm beginning to like this—before you know it you've got exponential growth! And they would *all* know, every last one of them, that if they didn't spread the word, the story would die. For it wouldn't be just the Boss's story anymore, it would be their story too and they would be right in the middle of it. They would be a new breed of messengers, getting ready to take over for us, farther down the road.

So who should go? What's that, Michael? Last time the message went to the common folk, so this time it should go to the world leaders? Well, so long as we remember that the *first* folks to hear were the shepherds, I like the idea of touching all the bases.

But let's be realistic for a moment. We'll have to think through all sorts of protocol problems. If it's world leaders, which world leader gets to go to the head of the line? Lots of room there for misunderstanding. Even trick-ier: Which world leader is sent to the foot of the line? And, trickiest of all, when they arrive at their destination, which one gets to be interviewed by Charlayne Hunter-Gault?

Yes, Raphael? Send a smaller symbolic number of leaders to represent the rest? Gotcha! Any particular symbolic number come to mind, Raphael? There's 3, of course, and 7, and 153, before we even get involved with square roots to the fourth power. But listen, gang. Time is short. For sim-plicity's sake, let's just leave it at three—the folks Upstairs are already breathing down our necks. Any objections? So ordered.

Next item: Transit. How do they get there? Considering that they'll need to travel at night as well as in the daytime to meet the Boss's sched-ule, we need help. Michael, why don't you ring up the Office of Celestial Navigation and see if they couldn't temporarily pull a few stars just a bit out of orbit to brighten the nighttime sky and show the leaders where they're going with all that endless trudging.

What's that, Raphael? Of *course* they'll be "trudging" on foot all the way. How else would you get them there? The airplane isn't going to be invented for two thousand years.

Camels? What do you mean, camels? . . . Camels! Ah, they'll be riding camels. Rafe, what a concept! Camels it is. Oh, the Boss is going to love this. And every kid who ever hears the story will be entranced. And besides, I'm told they're very economical. Three weeks on a single tankful of water.

Okay. We've got the concept, we've got the props. What about the plot-line? Let's clarify that a bit and then we can fax the whole thing Upstairs. Plotline . . . We need a conflict.

How about this? The three leaders, whether we call them kings or as-trologers or sages or inhabitants of Missouri or whatever, get close to the place where they are supposed to find the baby. Naturally, they all go to the nearest palace to pay their respects to the local potentate, right? Pro-tocol and all that . . . But (just to keep the suspense thing at a maximum) the local king is not glad to see them at all. They tell him they've come to worship a king, right? But when he says, "Here I am," *nobody kneels.* So he figures (you know how paranoid people in places of authority get), he fig-ures the whole thing is a plot to overthrow him. He is "greatly perturbed." But he can't admit that in front of a Secretary of State from a foreign coun-try. Such an admission of regal instability would be an open invitation for another country to invade and conquer. So he says to the visitors in an oily voice, something like, "When you find this king come back and tell me, so that I can go to worship him too." But our kings weren't born yester-day—the folks in Casting will give us the cream of the crop—and we know for sure that they'll get the word out not to darken Herod's door again, once they've bowed their way out.

It looks to me as though that is the high point of the story—the power politics played out in the king's court. If so, the rest of the script can unfold right on schedule. They find the barn outside Bethlehem, they kneel, they leave their gifts, they check out, they go back home, they spread the story around— and from then on the whole world knows that the Boss loves everyone.

Any leftover details? No, Michael, I don't think we have to give them names. With a story like this, the next generation of messengers will find people already beginning to name them. And I'll bet they give a good racial mix as well.

Uh, we've still got a gender absence here. But once again, let's count on the later tellers of the tale to make it better. Someday, instead of telling The Story of the Three Kings, somebody will start telling The Story of the Two Kings and a Queen, and later on it will be The Story of Two Queens and a King. And maybe someday they'll all be singing "We Three Queens of Orient Are." We start the story but we can't finally control it once it's been let loose in the world.

Okay? Okay. Feed it to the fax.

And now for some informal commentary. Change of mood, change of scene. But this is still Gabe, on the line, but off the record, speaking not in an angelic capacity but simply as someone who has the Boss's best interests at heart. Just between us, we were really pushed that day, getting it together to meet the celestial deadline. And now that the heat is off, I want to indicate a couple of things we maybe didn't highlight as much as we should have. Maybe when you retell the story you can fill in some of the blanks we left.

The main thing we didn't make clear enough (except in the heady encounter between Herod and the camel riders) is that the story isn't just about spiritual stuff. It's all tied up with things like economics and politics. I mean, *who was bowing to whom* in the manger scene? You can be sure the Boss wasn't giving accolades to the kings and sages, telling them what a fine job they were doing. Not at all. It was the other way around. The kings and sages were bowing to the Boss, meaning, "We know that we are under you, not above you. If your scheme is l-o-v-e, we've got to find ways to use our political and economic clout in the service of l-o-v-e." And that's about the most radical thing the Boss could possibly suggest to you earthlings.

So as you retell the story, try to get across that it's not so much the telling of a new story as *the enactment of an old story*—the story about folks who acknowledge that the first commandment of all is "You shall have no other Bosses before me." And that that's the Boss's consistent story, folks, whether on Sinai, or in Bethel, or in Babylon, or from a manger—or from a cross. It's always the same story, and the l-o-v-e part always has j-u-s-t-i-c-e smack-dab in the middle of it. Which puts the ball in your court.

Why do you suppose the Boss did this crazy thing of getting involved in the mess of your everyday life as earthlings? It seems to me (if you will pardon my utter frankness) that it is because you earthlings have made such a mess of things. There are folks around to l-o-v-e—and you exploit them. The Boss gives you a wonderful planet—and you are destroying the whole ecosystem. You make lines on a map between so-called countries and dare other people to step across them—and when they do you shoot them. The Boss has provided enough food for everyone—and you hoard it just for a few. The Boss has given you laws—and you break them. The Boss has sent prophets—and you call them mad.

So this time, the Boss doesn't just tell you something, the Boss *acts it out.* Not just a message about l-o-v-e, but a messenger who embodies l-o-v-e. Not just an exhortation about j-u-s-t-i-c-e, but an example of being just, modeling concern for the widows and orphans and all the other destitute in the world.

Face it, earthlings, the Boss has a special concern about the poor because you treat them so badly. Face it, earthlings, the shepherds got invited to the manger, first, and only after them the kings and potentates. Not the other way around. There's a pretty important message there somewhere.

The message seems to be that if you earthlings don't act out l-o-v-e and j-u-s-t-i-c-e, things will not go well with you. But when you *do,* it's peace and righteousness all over the place. So hear the word and come on board. What could be plainer?

Of course, the Boss still has one last resort available. That's to ask me to take up my horn and signal the end of the whole enterprise—what in the trade we call Doomsday. But it doesn't have to come to that. So hear the message again—for the first time.

O God, you've given us chances galore to hear your message. And now you've let us see it. Don't let us dismiss l-o-v-e and j-u-s-t-i-c-e as no more than interesting concepts to be thought about and then forgotten. Drive home to us by whatever means you choose a recognition that we are all in this thing together and that the best thing we have going for us is the fact that you are in the thick of it too. Thanks. In Jesus' name. Amen.

– 10 –

The Biblical Obsession with Food
(Ministry)

Reading: Mark 2:23–28
Text: One Sabbath [Jesus] was going through the cornfields; and
as they went along his disciples began to pluck ears of corn.—Mark
2:23

Most of Jesus' ministry was carried out in the northern part of Palestine, in
Galilee. He spent a great deal of time out of doors, and walked long distances
with his disciples. The lectionary reading illustrates how simple events become
fraught with meaning.

> One Sabbath [Jesus] was going through the cornfields; and as they went
> along his disciples began to pluck ears of corn. The Pharisees said to him,
> "Why are they doing what is forbidden on the Sabbath?" He answered,
> "Have you never read what David did when he and his men were hungry
> and had nothing to eat? He went into the house of God, in the time of Abi-
> athar the high priest, and ate the sacred bread, though no one but the priest
> is allowed to eat it, and even gave it to his men."
> He also said to them, "The Sabbath was made for people—not people for
> the Sabbath; so the Son of Man is in charge even of the Sabbath." (Mark
> 2:23–28)

Today is the first Sunday of the month. That means that we have a meal
around the Lord's Table, *inside* the church, and (it being also the date of
the annual church picnic) we then have a meal around a picnic table *outside* the church. Not only that, but the *scripture* reading is about . . . food.

Our Puritan ancestors would have called this providential. How fore-
sighted of God to arrange this triple focus on food! And how important for
the preacher to realize that whereas long after-dinner speeches are one of
the trials of the human condition, short speeches before dinner are okay.
So let me say something briefly about the meals we are about to have—the

59

meal around the Lord's Table, the meal around the picnic table—and the relationship between them.

But first, a word from our sponsor: "One Sabbath [Jesus] was going through the cornfields; and as they went along his disciples began to pluck ears of corn" (Mark 2:23). The two phrases that comprise this verse confound all our expectations. Look at them again.

"One Sabbath [Jesus] was going . . . " Going where? Since it is meticulously noted that the occasion is the Sabbath we can conjecture that the verse ought to continue, "One Sabbath he was going to the temple," or "One Sabbath he was going apart to pray, as his custom was," or, "One Sabbath he was going off to preach somewhere." Wherever he was going it would surely be in keeping with the religious solemnity of the day. But no. The only information provided is that "one Sabbath he was going through the cornfields," through the meadows, perhaps to meet some friends or have a picnic lunch.

This sense of letdown is sustained in the second half of the verse: "and as they went along [on the Sabbath] his disciples began to . . . " Began to . . . what? "Began to sing a hymn," or "began to recite a unison prayer," or, maybe even "began to spend the day fasting"? No. We are told, almost casually, that "As they went along his disciples began to pluck ears of corn." Why? A very simple reason. They were hungry.

I

Let us use this episode, which has many other levels of meaning, as *an illustration of how obsessed the Bible is with food,* which we usually think of as a secular rather than a holy thing. But start reading the Bible in terms of its emphasis on food, and you will be amazed.

You are hardly into Genesis before the matter of eating an apple in a garden has assumed center stage. Noah in the ark is hopeful when the dove brings back an olive branch. Olives? Ah, food must be close at hand. The main problem in the wanderings in the desert is where the food will come from—and fortunately manna is provided. The prophets make a big deal about having enough food, and an even bigger deal out of seeing to it that everybody else has enough food too. Central to the Lord's Prayer is the petition, "Give us this day our daily bread." When five thousand folks are off on a retreat with Jesus in the countryside, and it gets to be suppertime and there is no delicatessen for miles around, Jesus doesn't tell them to go without supper; he and all the folks together provide food for a gala picnic. And when he and his followers get together in a tense time in an upper room in Jerusalem, they don't have a strategy session, they have supper.

It's pretty apparent that the Bible isn't such a "spiritual" book that it glosses over such things as eating and drinking.

II

All of this tells us something very important concerning *the meal we share around the Lord's table.* The church calls this a holy meal, a sacred meal. It is the high point of the Roman Catholic and Orthodox liturgies, and (if we would but study our own history) was also meant to be the high point of Reformed worship as well, as John Calvin tried so hard and so unsuccessfully to persuade the less enlightened members of his session in Geneva. Both the Roman Catholic and Reformed traditions say that this meal brings us "the real presence of Christ." We mean different things when we use that phrase, but we both affirm that at this special table, Christ is present in a special way: for Catholics because something has happened to the very nature of the bread and wine, for Protestants because the very *act* of gathering together is itself the condition for Christ to be present—when two or three are gathered together in his name, he is with them. That doesn't mean we can't be one-on-one with Jesus, but the way he is most likely to touch our lives is through other people, in community.

So there is something special, something holy, about this event. Goethe wrote that "the highest cannot be spoken; it can only be acted." Here in the pulpit I can *speak about* the "real presence of Christ," but at the table we open ourselves to *experiencing* the "real presence of Christ." So it is important that we act this out by physically gathering around his table together.

It is high and holy, all right, but more than slightly mystifying. How can we make sense of it? Only, I think, by reflecting on something that has not so far been mentioned. The only way the meal "works" is because we bring into the church, and set on the table, and *use,* not sacred things we can't understand, but *ordinary* things that we can understand: food and drink, bread and wine. What we need for a sense of God's presence is exactly what we need for the survival of our bodies. If there is no food or drink, there is no sacrament. So if something special happens at this table, it is possible only because we have brought the most prosaic stuff of our everyday experience, food and drink. We can't have the special without the ordinary.

III

Take a look now at *the meal around the picnic table.* There we will be focusing less on "the real presence of Christ" and more on the real presence of one another: David, Christine, Jody, Judy, Jeremy, Peter, Diana, Derrick,

Jeff, Will, Craig, Miriam, and (if I may cite a name that is suddenly the cultural rage) Bob. At the picnic table we are celebrating one another, rejoicing in the fact that we cherish one another, and that we can have—if I may employ theological terminology—one hell of a good time joking, sharing, listening, playing, eating, and drinking. We are using the same basic things so crucial to our earlier meal around the Lord's table—food and drink, this time in the form of sandwiches, hot dogs, Chardonnay and Diet Coke. And we do much the same thing at the picnic table and the Lord's table; we eat and drink but with a reverse twist: just as the "holy" meal has meaning because of the use of ordinary things, so this ordinary picnic meal has meaning because of the use of "holy" things, such as the recognition we bring from the Lord's table that we are all forgiven sinners, that we can love each other even if sometimes we don't like each other very much, that just as Christ's real presence in the holy meal makes us conscious of the real presence of each other around the Lord's table, so the presence of each other around the picnic table makes us conscious of the presence of Christ, who is with us on so-called ordinary occasions, just as he is on so-called special occasions.

IV

So how do the two meals relate to one another? Here I must employ a theological stratagem—the declaration of a "dialectic," which means here "a complicated relationship." I think we have to say as Christians that the *two meals are very like one another, even as they are also very unlike one another.* Both things are true, but since our tradition has always concentrated on the unlikenesses, let me focus in conclusion on the likenesses.

The meal inside the church we call a holy meal, but part of its purpose is surely to remind us that *every* meal can be a holy meal, a meal where everyone is accepted, where there is food for all, where we know that we can only be what the Bible calls "in Christ" if we are "in community." We are probably more aware of the presence of Christ at the Lord's table than at the picnic table, and more aware of the sacredness of other persons at the picnic table than we are at the Lord's table—which means finally that since those views by themselves are deficient, we need to affirm that the picnic table is the Lord's table, and the Lord's table is also the picnic table. Each reinforces the other. Both meals are meant to draw us closer both to God and to one another. And we need both of them for our full spiritual nourishing.

If you don't feel the "real presence of Christ' in church this morning, take heart. Maybe you will feel that presence at the picnic this afternoon when some eight-year-old unexpectedly comforts a three-year-old who got knocked over wandering across the volleyball court; or when someone you strongly disagreed with at Adult Study says, "I'm sure we're not as far apart as it seemed. Let's talk"; or when you feel closer to another person than you did earlier simply because of the way the sun caught his or her face for a moment. And in these and other ways we can be filled with a sense of the goodness God offers us in the most apparently insignificant things, and discover, at the picnic table, what it means when the liturgies for the other table encourage us "to feed on Christ in our hearts by faith with thanksgiving."

So let's not allow the meals shared at the picnic table, and the dining room table, and the kitchen table, and the Lord's table to become too remote from one another. They are all means of grace to bind us more closely to God and to one another.

O God, you are present to us in many ways and in many places. Help us to be on the lookout for you in every place, and dare to believe that you might confront us where we least expect you. Let our meals at various tables remind us of your love for us, so that we can be channels of that love to others. In Jesus' name we pray. Amen.

– 11 –
Mary and Martha:
A Conundrum
(Ministry)

Reading: Luke 10:38–42
Text: While they were on their way, Jesus came to a village—Luke
10:38 (the only noncontroversial verse in the entire passage)

"This is a woman's story," I was prepared to argue with Diana, my ministerial colleague, "you take it." But then I realized that she would surely have responded, with both logic and hierarchical authority on her side, that that was a very good reason for me to have to struggle with it. I emerged from this imaginary conversation with a very clear conviction that she should accept the assignment for the next Superbowl Sunday.

So listen to a controversial passage from that section of Luke's Gospel when Jesus has set his face toward Jerusalem and is brewing up stormy receptions along the way. Luke surely meant the episode as a respite from the external battles. But, as we shall see, it has generated both external and internal battles of its own. Luke writes:

> While they were on the way, Jesus came to a village where a woman named Martha made him welcome. She had a sister, Mary, who seated herself at Jesus' feet and stayed there listening to his words.
> Now Martha was distracted by her many tasks, so she came to Jesus and said, "Do you not care that my sister has left me to get on with the work by myself? Tell her to come and give me a hand." But Jesus answered, "Martha, Martha, you are fretting and fussing about so many things; only one thing is necessary. Mary has chosen what is best; it shall not be taken away from her." (Luke 10:38–42)

A quick perusal of the church directory produces eight to a dozen Marys among our membership, depending on whether we count Marianne (one word), Mary Alice (two words), and minor variants from the original, like Marion, Maria, Marietta, and a "hidden" Mary, the actual first name of one we know ordinarily as Judy. In the passage we have just heard, the Marys are the winners.

A similar perusal of the church directory reveals only four Marthas. According to the passage we have just heard, it's better to be a Mary (however you pronounce it) than a Martha, for the Marthas are the losers.

Anybody who knows our own Marthas knows that any division in which they end up on the minus side of the ledger is nonsense. And I mention this local lore only to make the point that on whatever level we approach this story of Mary and Martha, we face a conundrum, which the dictionary defines as "any puzzling question or problem." This story has more than its share of puzzling questions or problems.

I

Transpose the scene for a moment to our own time. Jesus is sitting in the living room talking to Mary, who hangs on every word of the Master with the same kind of adoring glance a recent President's wife used to bestow on her master. Martha, by contrast, is in the kitchen banging pots and pans around and sending an obvious message to Mary, still in the living room, that Mary willfully ignores. Finally, realizing that subtlety will get her nowhere, especially when punctuated by pots and pans, Martha storms into the living room and says—to Jesus, not to Mary—something like, "Look, I'm trying to prepare a sit-down meal for fourteen people, who are due here in exactly an hour and a half, and I can't possibly get it done by myself. For heaven's sake, Jesus, won't you ask Mary to come and give me a hand? I can't get a rise out of her. Maybe she'll listen to you."

Now in our culture, with the best possible cast of characters, Jesus might respond something like this: "Look, why don't Mary and I both come out to the kitchen and give you a hand, and then we can all work and talk together." To which Martha might respond, "Great! Or better still, Jesus, why don't you just do your loaves and fishes thing, and then we won't have to stay in the kitchen at all."

In Luke's version, however, Jesus responds by appearing to scold Martha and praise Mary.

So what, then, are some of the conundrums or perplexities within the story itself and the way we approach it? The male-oriented commentaries of my seminary days are an interesting case study. They refer to the passage as "an exquisite tale," "a charming vignette," in which they perceive the role of women receiving special attention.

I have discovered, however, that the perception of most women today is that this is not an exquisite tale at all, nor is it a charming vignette, but is rather one more example of a biblical attempt to put women down and give rewards to dutiful subservience of women to men. Rather than increasing feminine solidarity it creates a conflict between these two women: one of them wins, one of them loses.

Our problems with the text, in other words, are not just in the text itself, but in the perceptions we bring to the text.

The Women's Bible Commentary itemizes other concerns. The story appears to reward passivity and meekness, exalt contemplation over action, and offer women a model of a rather shy and gentle Mary who is to be emulated by readers, rather than championing an aggressive and vigorous Martha. Even if it is acknowledged that Luke has a higher view of women than the other Gospels, we discover, on reflection, that this isn't saying a great deal. Women are seen as admirable if they know their place, which is in the kitchen, provided they don't complain; or sitting silently at the feet of a man, provided they do not ask probing questions. And in all this Luke is not being personally invidious, but simply reflecting the biases of any first-century man, living in a world that allowed only a very subordinate role for women within its social, political, and economic milieu.

When later Christians wanted to delineate the two chief modes of Christian behavior, they settled on contemplation *or* action, pitting them against each other, either one *or* the other but not both, and Mary and Martha were stereotypical examples already to hand. Mary turns away from daily chores to meditate with Jesus, her back to the open kitchen door, while Martha has no time for such nonsense and becomes the Ms. Social Activist of the Bethany Christian Church Women's Endeavor Society. This tidy scheme actually subverts and destroys the true nature of Christian living, which insists that you can't be just a "Mary" or just a "Martha," inner-directed or outer-directed, contemplative or gung ho activist. Hard as it is, you have to be both.

II

All of this seems to leave us at an impasse. How can we possibly learn from a story susceptible to such different readings?

The only honest way to deal with this question is to realize that the Mary-Martha story illustrates in microcosm what is true of the entire biblical story in macrocosm. Let us try to illustrate this by an analogy.

We Christians believe that in Jesus of Nazareth, God indwelt a fully human life as much as could be done without overriding that full humanity. That means, among other things, that Jesus had a first-century view of the world: he spoke Aramaic, not King James English; he thought David wrote all the psalms (which he didn't); and he expected his own immanent return to rule in glory. He did not know about the internal combustion machine, space probes to Mars, or what goes on inside the head of H. Ross Perot. The early church clung to this belief in the full humanity of Jesus against a minority who tried to claim that Jesus only seemed to be human and that his humanity was a fake.

Now we have to make much the same kind of assertion about the Bible. We assert that in the Bible, God speaks a special kind of word to us that we don't find anywhere else. And just as Jesus was a fully human being (whatever else he was), so the Bible is a fully human book (whatever else it is). This means that the Bible has a worldview molded by the Hebraic and Greek culture within which it was written. Its writers accept that culture without serious question, including a patriarchal point of view that takes male superiority for granted. Its writers do not know about universal human suffrage and would be utterly flabbergasted at the notion of a senator named Barbara Boxer.

Notice that this stress on the full humanity of Jesus, and on the book that tells about him, is a *plus* rather than a minus. It persuades us that God really takes us seriously in our here-and-nowness, by using that same here-and-nowness to communicate with us—through a human life and a human book.

The consequence of all this is that we are given an exciting and even dangerous kind of freedom in approaching the Bible and using it. Not every verse or chapter or book is of equal importance. And within this account of God's confronting us through human writers, the insights of those human writers are always subject to question. They are not passive conduits through whom God directly dictates a script without errors. Sometimes they tell us that it is God's will that we slay every man, woman, and child of the enemy captured in battle (1 Sam. 15:3). Sometimes they affirm that war is the ultimate obscenity and that we can never participate in it. Both themes are there, and we have to choose between them.

The writers also use the instruments of the culture they are addressing, to communicate fully to that culture. To Greeks, the uniqueness of Jesus is suggested by the story of a virgin birth—a very common concept if you are a first-century Greek. But to first-century Jews, the uniqueness of Jesus is suggested by demonstrating how he fulfills Old Testament prophecy. If these images do not speak to us, it doesn't mean that the uniqueness of Jesus, to which they are pointing, goes down the tubes; it simply means that we have to find images in our own time and place that communicate uniqueness to us. God will use whatever means are at hand. As W. H. Auden wrote after the Roman Catholics decided to translate the Latin mass into the vernacular, "The Holy Ghost does not abhor a golfer's jargon." Right on!

So we have to discriminate within the biblical materials.

III

This brings us back to Mary and Martha. There are certainly parts of the story that do not help us to a better understanding of God's will. We must put them aside, so that we can then see more clearly what is left to affirm. Here are some warning flags I would raise; yours may be different.

We must discard any interpretations of the Mary-Martha story that pits women against each other, in which one wins while the other loses, as though men were referees to decide how women should use their lives.

We must discard any attempts to make people fit stereotypical patterns ("She's a 'Mary'," or "There's that 'Martha' side coming out again,") just as we must discard similar attempts to categorize men by, let us say, their percentage of "iron in the belly."

We must discard interpretations of this story that freeze social customs into a first-century mode, suggesting, for example, that men have no possible role in the kitchen or that women should never be those who teach but only (at best) those who are taught.

With these things (and perhaps more) set aside, what can still be salvaged, or, to put it more felicitously, what can we still affirm from this story?

We will need always to relate it to the other stories about Mary and Martha, which give us further materials with which to work. Mary continues to do pretty well, not only in the other Gospels but in the Christian tradition as a whole. But in fairness to the contemporary Marthas, who don't get much consolation from the Luke passage, it should be pointed out that even in the New Testament Martha makes a spectacular leap forward. In the Fourth Gospel, written perhaps thirty years after Luke, it is not Mary, but Martha, who makes the definitive declaration that Jesus is the Messiah (John 11:27). That is a nice rounding out of the circle: Martha, the pots and pans lady, who in Luke was *not* the one sitting at Jesus' feet, is the one who delivers the ultimate confession of faith about him. And the later tradition gives yet another accolade to Martha: there is a whole group of stories suggesting that it was Martha, and not St. George, who really slew the dragon.

On now to some reclaiming. As far as *Mary* is concerned, Gustavo Gutiérrez has reminded us that we can affirm a radical breakthrough on Jesus' part in relation to Mary, for when he admitted her to what we would call a theological discussion, such an action, in that era, was virtually unthinkable. Women were carefully excluded from the circles of learning. "Better the Torah be burnt," one aphorism went, "than that it be explained to a woman." But Jesus overturns such accepted customs: Mary is welcome. And that tells us that we, too, in our time, are to challenge encrusted religious traditions that are taken for granted, by refusing to abide by them. Not a bad rationale for congregations struggling toward the acknowledgment in our denomination of full equality for gays and lesbians.

We can also affirm the radical breakthrough on Jesus' part in relation to *Martha*, in making clear to her that she didn't have to stay in the kitchen, as the culture of the time insisted that she do, but could come out and, along with Mary, do something entirely different. This is an invitation to women today, or any persons who feel themselves unfairly confined in situations that are unfulfilling, to break loose.

We can affirm the new possibilities that emerge for *both Mary and Martha*. Mary in the story is simply passively sitting at Jesus' feet, saying not a word, being what we might today call a good girl. But that is not yet real education. Only as Mary feels free to break in, to question, to challenge, can real learning take place. Fat chance, you may think, but in the Fourth Gospel this same Mary has learned enough to stand up to Jesus and to *criticize* him for not arriving in time to save her brother Lazarus's life (John 11:32). Martha, in the story, is liberated from being compelled to work in the kitchen, and is reminded that if she chooses to spend time in the kitchen, fussing and fretting don't need to be part of the agenda. No need for a big production every time a wandering rabbi comes for a visit. No need to get bowled over by a bunch of details.

Finally, we can affirm that all of us need to participate in both the life of contemplation (symbolized by Mary sitting at Jesus' feet) and the life of action (symbolized by Martha among the pots and pans), and that to disdain either is to run the risk of, on the one hand, pious irrelevance, and, on the other hand, destructive burnout.

IV

Those are just a few starters. Take the story home and reflect further on what must be discarded or salvaged—affirmed—in your own life.

Let our text (which makes an appearance only in the last paragraph) be the starting point: "While they were on their way, Jesus came to a village." Take it from there and see what happens.

O God, you don't exactly make things easy for us, but at least you don't leave them dull. Give us the gift of discernment, so that we can sift through what is important to us in this and other stories, so that our love for you and for one another can increase to the heights of your glory and the depths of our commitment. In Jesus' name. Amen.

– 12 –
"So What Happened Next?"
(The Transfiguration)
A Dialogue Sermon with Sydney T. Brown

Reading: Luke 9:18–36 and Luke 9:37–43
Text: They were all struck with awe at the greatness of God.
—Luke 9:43

The story of the transfiguration is reported in considerable detail in all three of the Synoptic Gospels: Matthew, Mark, and Luke. The disciples and Jesus are at a crisis point in Jesus' ministry. Things have not been going well and they have been up north near Caesarea Philippi, taking stock of their situation. They are now on their way south to Jerusalem where they anticipate a fateful encounter with both the religious and secular authorities. Jesus has apparently decided that a few of them, himself included, need a little extra fortification for the upcoming struggle. Luke picks it up from there:

About a week after this he took Peter, John, and James and went up a mountain to pray. And while he was praying the appearance of his face changed and his clothes became dazzling white. Suddenly there were two men talking with him—Moses and Elijah—who appeared in glory and spoke of his departure, the destiny he was to fulfill in Jerusalem. Peter and his companions had been overcome by sleep; but when they awoke they saw his glory and the two men who stood beside him. As these two were moving away from Jesus, Peter said to him, "Master, it is good that we are here. Shall we make three shelters, one for you, one for Moses, and one for Elijah?"; but he spoke without knowing what he was saying. As he spoke there came a cloud which cast its shadow over them; they were afraid as they entered the cloud, and from it a voice spoke: "This is my Son, my Chosen; listen to him." After the voice had spoken, Jesus was seen to be alone. The disciples kept silence and did not at that time say a word to anyone of what they had seen. (Luke 9:28–36)

RMB (*completing the lectionary reading*): Here ends the Gospel lesson.
STB: So?

70

RMB: What do you mean, "So"?

STB: So *what happened next?*

RMB: What do you mean, "What happened next?" That's the end of the story.

STB: I still want to know what happened next. If that's the whole story, it's a cop-out. A big event takes place and then, as Luke says in a moment of rare candor, nobody will even talk about it.

RMB: Listen. What does it take to satisfy you? Here is a very religious story from a time of great stress. Jesus and Peter and James and John go up a mountain and have a real experience of the presence of God. They do a little processing of the experience, and it's so . . . holy they don't even dare talk about it, for fear of spoiling it.

STB: You call *that* a plotline?

RMB: Sure. Look what it's got: religious experience on a wide screen. Not just prayers and visions, but human frailty as well (what Luke would have called sin if he'd been a Presbyterian), when Peter and James and John fall asleep in the midst of what the scholars call an epiphany. And then there's human recovery as well (what Luke would have called redemption if he'd been a Methodist). And Peter is so impressed he wants to stay up there permanently, and keep his heart strangely warmed. There's even a voice from heaven with a lesson in Christology. No wonder they were awestruck and couldn't talk about it. What more could you possibly want in a Bible passage?

STB (*making a tremendous effort to be patient*): Let me try again. I want to know *what happened next.* What did they *do* with all this? No consequences? No follow-through? No reflection on the comparison of before and after? No thinking that they've got to live differently? You can't just stay indefinitely in a state of religious fervor.

RMB: Peter certainly thought they could. He didn't want to let the vision fade away. Remember what he said?

STB: I certainly do! He said, "This has been great! Let's keep it alive. Let's build a retreat center right here, with cabins for Jesus and Moses and Elijah." Can't you see it? People coming every weekend to get away from the pressure and the turmoil down below, leaving all the mess of trying to make a living or get along with disagreeable neighbors. Up on the mountaintop they could have guided meditation, hymn singing, sunsets, and even workshops with Moses and Elijah. And always the hope that there might once again be a voice from heaven.

RMB: Well I must say, this knocking of religious experience seems to me in pretty poor taste in the middle of a Sunday morning worship service.

STB: I'm *not* "knocking religious experience" as you so delicately put it. I'm only knocking the notion that what we have just heard is the *whole* of religious experience, something that takes place *only* on a mountaintop, in a far-off place. So let me ask for the third, and I hope final, time, what . . . happened . . . next?

RMB: Well, the lectionary stops there. That's the end of the story.

STB: But it's not the end of Luke's Gospel, which, as I remember, goes on for quite a few more pages. What . . .

RMB: . . . happened next?

STB: Ah! At last we are beginning to communicate.

RMB: What happened next? I'm glad you asked that question. Let's see what happened next. Here we are: Luke 9:37–43. And it's a brand-new story:

Next day when they came down from the mountain a large crowd came to meet him. A man in the crowd called out, "Teacher, I implore you to look at my son, my only child. From time to time a spirit seizes him and with a sudden scream throws him into convulsions so that he foams at the mouth; it keeps on tormenting him and can hardly be made to let him go. I begged your disciples to drive it out, but they could not." Jesus answered, "What an unbelieving and perverse generation! How long shall I be with you and endure you? Bring your son here." But before the boy could reach him the demon dashed him to the ground and threw him into convulsions. Jesus spoke sternly to the unclean spirit, cured the boy, and gave him back to his father. And they were all struck with awe at the greatness of God.

STB: All right! Now we're getting somewhere. That's *not* a brand-new story at all, as you call it. That is simply the completion of the lectionary story. They didn't just stay up there on the mountain, perpetuating spiritual bliss. They went back down again, and the really important thing is what they did when they got back down.

RMB: I'd lay odds that Peter started getting people to invest in building a retreat center, complete with a very favorable first mortgage.

STB: As I heard it, Luke is pretty silent about Peter's activity. But he is very up-front about Jesus' activity. And what is that?

RMB: Well, Jesus immediately gets involved in healing an epileptic boy. It's so . . . unexpected and jarring. After all that serenity on the mountaintop, all that sense of God's presence, all of a sudden we're dealing with a boy who needs medical help. I think we ought to keep the two stories separate.

STB: You're making the point in spite of yourself. Ecstasy and epilepsy do belong together in the story. The vision and the valley cannot be separated, any more than spirituality and justice can be separated. And the disciples couldn't handle it any better than you are handling it. What does Jesus do? Fresh from that mountaintop he tackles the first thing at hand, which is a child of God, and even more explicitly a child of God *in need*. And if a mountaintop experience has the result of giving you a religious excuse to ignore a child of God in need, then so much the worse for mountaintop experiences.

RMB (*definitely on the defensive*): I'm *not* talking about ignoring children in need. Who can quarrel with the idea of dealing with the implications of a religious experience?

STB: I can! Because you've got it all wrong. You are saying that *religious* experiences like prayer and visions happen only on mountaintops and that *secular* things like epilepsy happen down in the valley. That's a trickle-down theory of religion, and it's no better theologically than it is economically.

RMB: I still don't think they fit together.

STB: They *do* fit together, or, better still, they are two parts of the same thing. And if your skeptical soul still isn't satisfied, and you still disagree, I appeal to Luke. Look again at the conclusion of the passage you just read.

RMB: You mean the reaction of the crowd after the healing?

STB: I mean the reaction of the crowd after the healing.

RMB: Well, it says, "And all were astonished . . . "

STB: Astonished at what? Was it astonishment at the aggressiveness of the boy's father asking a favor from the wandering rabbi? Was it astonishment at the frightening scene of the demon coming onstage and attacking the boy? Was it astonishment at the unwillingness of the disciples to deal with the issue? What were they astonished *at*?

RMB: Well, actually, it says, "And they were all struck with awe at the greatness of God."

STB: *Thank you,* St. Luke. Don't you find it rather interesting that during the entire part of the story on the mountaintop, with all the voices and visions and clouds and appearances, *never once* are all those so-called religious things described as examples of the "greatness of God"? When Luke wants to describe the majesty of God what does he do? He does it by describing an act of healing, in an encounter that is, as you said so well, "jarring," an experience we'd just as soon have skipped. In my book, that's a *real* religious experience—relating the mountaintop to what is happening in the immediate ordinary world, surrounded by immediate and ordinary folks. That's where Luke shows the "greatness of God," becoming visible, in an incredible miracle of setting free.

RMB: Well, suppose, for the sake of argument (but just for the sake of argument), that you are right, and that what you have just been saying made sense in biblical times to people who were used to visions and miracles and voices from heaven, and who weren't sophisticated enough to sort out what happened in heaven and what happened on earth. It made a good story for those times. But we live in the twentieth century, and we know that you have to distinguish the sacred from the secular, spirituality from justice, and all that. It just clouds the issue to try to connect them today, the way you are doing.

STB: Okay, if St. Luke won't convince you, let me appeal to our own experience. Remember the service we attended in the Philippines immediately on our arrival, when the entire two-hour liturgy was in the Tagalog dialect?

RMB: Can I ever forget? Two hours of not having a clue about what was going on.

STB: Right. And in your restless examination and reexamination of the printed order of worship, you could find only one word in the whole program that you could clearly identify. It was the Tagalog word for "holy."

RMB: I remember. And the Tagalog word for "holy"—and this really rocked me—was spelled b-a-n-a-l—banal. That made no sense. The holy and the banal should be opposites—two different things.

STB: That's what you thought then. But the subsequent discovery we both made in the Philippines was that there, the holy—the manifestation of God—was found right *in the midst* of the banal, the ordinary, the obvious. The holy was present in people taking risks, groups working for justice, providing help to AIDS victims, women engaged in ministry to prostitutes at the U.S. military bases, congregational interventions to the government for the release of the wrongly imprisoned. It was in the midst of the stuff of everyday life, the banal, that you and I (who are hardly creatures of "Bible times") found what Luke describes as "the greatness of God." And *we* were "struck with awe at the greatness of God," just as they were. And our struggle now is to make the connections here at home that were so clear in the Philippines as well as in Jesus' time:

> Connecting the wonder of the spiritual experience to the very down-to-earth realities of our daily life.
> Getting kids dressed, breakfasted, off to school or child care.
> Existing in some kind of positive relationship to the person next to us at work.
> Working to change our immigration laws so that the strangers in our land, the helpers in our homes, don't live in fear of being deported.

We need to become more adept at connecting the inner journey and the outer journey, so that the one fortifies us for the other, so that our work in the community and the public realm is enriched by the life of the spirit and that our spiritual life is enriched, informed, and grounded in the actualities of our struggle for justice in the community.

We must learn to live more easily with our prayers for each other here in church around the Communion table, *and* our "calls to act" when we leave church. The calls are our invitation to each other to be involved with and to support each other, as we move from the circle of our lives here in church to the ordinary, yes, the banal world in which we live, just as we need to come from those involvements to be enriched and nourished by our gathering together around our common table here in church.

RMB: Much as it hurts me to say so, I'm beginning to see your point. You're saying that what happens to the people like us is just like what happened when Jesus and Peter and James and John came down from the mountaintop into the ordinary world of the banal, and found the majesty of God right there themselves.

STB: You're a fast learner.

RMB (*reflectively*): Gosh, that's quite a story. I wonder what happened next?

STB: Hey! That's *my* line.

O God, we always seem to want to carve out a bit of impregnable space where we can go and be "religious" and get away from all the evil and the compromise and the deceit. Deny us that distortion, and show us where the signs of your presence truly are, in the banal as well as the beautiful, in the midst of engagement and concern, and help us to pull it all together so that there is no time when we are really separated from you or from any of your children. In Jesus' name. Amen.

Holy Week according to CBS and NPR, or Dan Rather and Robert MacNeil Cover the Jerusalem Beat (Palm Sunday and Good Friday)

Reading: Mark 11:1–11

Mark devotes more than half of his Gospel to the events of the last week of Jesus' life. In the other Gospels as well, the proportions are impressive. For the early church, what happened in that particular Passover Week was clearly the heart of the story. The reading from Mark is straightforward and is the earliest material we have about the events under consideration.

> They were now approaching Jerusalem, and when they reached Bethpage and Bethany, close by the Mount of Olives, he sent off two of his disciples. "Go into the village opposite," he told them, "and just as you enter you will find tethered there a colt which no one has yet ridden. Untie it and bring it here. If anyone asks why you are doing this, say, "The Master needs it, and will send it back here without delay." So they went off, and found the colt tethered beside a door outside in the street. As they were untying it, some of the bystanders asked, "What are you doing, untying the colt?" They answered as Jesus had told them, and were then allowed to take it. So they brought the colt to Jesus, and when they had spread their cloaks on it he mounted it. Many people carpeted the road with their cloaks, while others spread greenery which they had cut in the fields; and those in front and those behind shouted, "Hosanna! Blessed is he who comes in God's name. Blessed is the realm of our father David which is coming. Hosanna in the heavens!"
>
> He entered Jerusalem and went into the temple. He looked around at everything; then, as it was already late, he went out to Bethany with the Twelve. (Mark 11:1–11)

Palm Sunday

Good evening. Dan Rather reporting directly from Jerusalem. Word was received here late today that a public demonstration against Herod had been organized by a group of Jews from Galilee, seeking to take advantage of the unrest during the Passover season.

With me in the studio is General Goliath, great-great-great-great-grandson of a lieutenant colonel who was felled in combat by an ancestor of today's demonstrators. General Goliath, tell us first of all just what *is* this Passover to which everyone keeps referring?

GOLIATH: Well, it's not a part of my own religion, but here in the Middle East we have to understand the religion of every potential enemy. Passover is a big religious event for the Hebrewites—as I believe they are called—celebrating their release from captivity in Egypt long ago.

RATHER: Isn't that more political than religious?

GOLIATH: Well, if you had studied the Hebrewites as much as I have had to, sir, you'd know that they don't really distinguish between religious and political events. They think their God wants them to be politically and economically free and not just (as some of them say) "spiritually" free. Makes *our* job a lot tougher. We have to be prepared for trouble whenever they get together, because, like I say, a religious feast like Passover is also a political celebration of their victory over Caesar (excuse me, over *Pharaoh*), and they might just try to go for it again. So it's twenty-four-hour alert as far as my security forces are concerned.

RATHER: One last question, General. What further steps have been taken to contain the uprising?

GOLIATH (*obviously quoting from the military officers handbook*): Sir, "military regulations prohibit my giving any information that might be of aid and comfort to the enemy."

RATHER: I quite understand, General, and I withdraw the question. Thank you for talking to us.

Ladies and gentlemen, we have just learned that there was an uprising in the center of Jerusalem earlier today. First, let's hear from Leslie Stahl, who has been covering these events at Herod's palace. What's the response up there at the palace, Leslie?

STAHL: Well, Dan, Herod has clearly decided to keep a low profile on this one. To him it's an internal dispute between Jewish factions and he doesn't want to appear to be taking sides. Just a few minutes ago David Gergin said there would be no official comment.

RATHER: Thank you, Leslie. We have the Chief of Protocol for the Roman Empire here in the studio. Tell us, Mr. Gaius, would someone making a triumphal entry ordinarily do so (as we've been told) on a donkey?

GAIUS: Not at all, sir. It's always done on white horses. The whole thing today was strictly small-town stuff. The Galilean fellow hadn't even gotten a parade permit. We may not even press charges.

RATHER: Thank you, Mr. Gaius. And now for some reactions from people in the crowd. Ray Brady is there.

BRADY: Thank you, Dan. I have one of Mr. Gaius's employees here, Dan. Mr. Zechariah, just what *is* your job with the Bureau of Triumphal Entries?

ZECHARIAH: I'm supposed to see that things go according to plan, that the crowd doesn't get out of hand, things like that. Of course, we have a lot of plainclothesmen mingling at all times to keep things orderly. It's what we call crowd control.

BRADY: And did you have any trouble this afternoon, Mr. Zechariah?

ZECHARIAH: Well, for a while it was touch and go, if you get my meaning. All of a sudden this unauthorized—and I want to stress the word "unauthorized"—demonstration begins to take place. No white horses, no bands, no official permits, just a bunch of people from the boondocks, throwing palms down on the ground while somebody went by on a donkey. Happily for us, nobody was drunk and nobody was smashing windows. I doubt anyone who wasn't there will even know there *was* a demonstration.

BRADY: Thank you, Mr. Zechariah. Dan, Mr. Micah here is in charge of the Sanitation Squad. Mr. Micah, how would you rank this demonstration in relation to other demonstrations you've cleaned up after?

MICAH: On a scale of ten, about a three. Since this wasn't an official triumphal entry we had only a skeleton crew on duty—it being holiday time and all that—so my men are going to be up half the night cleaning up those damn palm leaves. As far as I am concerned, the whole thing is one big nuisance.

BRADY: Thank you, Mr. Micah. Back to you, Dan.

RATHER: I'd like to put a question to Mr. Micah. Mr. Micah, all over town we've been hearing what those of us in the trade call Messiah-talk. It's a theory that sometime the Hebrewites (I believe that's what General Goliath called them) will find a leader who will set them free. Do you people at the grass roots put any stock in such rumors?

MICAH: Well, if folks think that what happened here just a few hours ago is supposed to be the coming of a Messiah, they've gotten their toes burned real bad.

RATHER: Thank you, Mr. Micah, for that frank appraisal. So far, I believe our early polls support your position. And now, back to Herod's palace, once more. Leslie, what's the latest word on the official attitude toward the rebellion?

STAHL: Dan, Marlin Fitzwater just met with reporters asking questions about the rebellion, and his only comment was, "What rebellion?" That about sums up official reaction as of now.

RATHER: Thank you, Leslie. And that just about wraps it up, ladies and gentlemen: Reports of an immanent takeover by a group of out-of-towners seem to have been highly exaggerated. When we return, "Prospects for a Peaceful Passover Week." But first, these messages . . .

Good Friday

Good evening, I'm Robert MacNeil. Leading the news this Friday night: the insurgency movement led by a young Galilean peasant, Joshua bar Josef, came to an end today. We have three experts with us this evening to assess the meaning of the weeklong uprising that began last Sunday. But first, this backgrounder from Charlayne Hunter-Gault, who has been on the scene all week. Charlayne . . .

CHARLAYNE: Robin, what appears to be the end of an insurgent uprising took place this afternoon when the leader Joshua bar Josef of Nazareth was executed on a dump heap outside the city wall. It's been a week full of intrigue, as the authorities have tried to contain a movement that at first they wanted to ignore, and yet a movement that increasingly threatened them as the week went on. Each day the leader of the insurgents has challenged both the religious and the political establishments in a series of explosive encounters. On Monday he confronted the religious authorities, charging that they were profaning the temple by selling animals for ritual slaughter within it. The temple police were summoned when Joshua angrily upset the tables of the money changers, and went after what he called the profaners with a whip, claiming, as he said, that they had "turned a house of prayer into a den of robbers."

All week there have been brisk encounters and exchanges and heckling in the streets, particularly when Joshua allegedly challenged the authority of Caesar by urging people not to give to Caesar what should only be given to God. By Wednesday evening, both the religious and secular authorities were plotting his arrest and execution. After Joshua's group had celebrated the Passover meal on Thursday evening, they went to the Mount of Olives, where soldiers were already waiting to arrest Joshua. Unconfirmed reports claim that one of the members of Joshua's group defected, and provided authorities with detailed information that made Joshua's arrest almost routine. Throughout Thursday night, interrogations of Joshua took place in various parts of the city, and by sunup it was determined that he was a threat to Caesar. After he had been worked over by the local police with billy clubs in what the police chief later said was an "aberration of policy" he was sentenced to be nailed to a cross until dead. Reliable witnesses report that he died three hours later at what is called the Place of a Skull. His followers have temporarily gone into hiding, although the Committee on Un-Roman Activities has promised an All Points Alert in an effort to apprehend them.

MACNEIL: Thank you. We now turn to our three experts who have different assessments of the events: General Goliath, head of the coalition security

forces for Herod who frequently appears on this program; Ms. Rebecca, an or-
ganizer for the homeless in Jerusalem; and Mr. Bartholomew, a member of
the band that had gathered around Joshua. For understandable reasons, Mr.
Bartholomew is not in the studio with us, but is hiding at a place known only
to our technician, who has arranged for audio, but not video, reception.

General Goliath, you first. How do you assess the events of the past week?

GOLIATH: We thought at first that this was just another run-of-the-mill
uprising, and that it would burn itself out in two or three days. But the
leader proved harder to nail (if you'll pardon the expression) than we had
expected. He had enough friends in the Passover crowds so that we couldn't
apprehend him publicly without incurring negative approval. Some of our
smartest operatives asked him very sophisticated questions in front of
large crowds, and for an uneducated man he was quick and able on his
feet. But after the blasphemy of suggesting that his God was greater than
Caesar, we immediately activated Operation Messiah-Trap. We had infil-
trated his group, bribed one of his followers to rat on him, so on Thursday
night he walked right into our arms on the Mount of Olives, just where
the informer had said he would be, right on schedule. It was a very clean
and efficient operation. I understand the man is now dead. Jerusalem will
be a safer place without him.

MACNEIL: Ms. Rebecca, I believe you have a different assessment of Joshua
bar Josef.

REBECCA: I think Roman law gives me the leeway to say that we, the common people, heard him gladly. His message gave us great encouragement;
he was preaching "good news to the poor . . . liberty to the captives," and
those are the people I work with every day. We all took hope from Joshua's
words and his deeds. He didn't just talk a good line, he lived it. He wasn't
an "expert on the problems of poor people," he was one of the poor people himself. I deal with the homeless, and that's what he was. By his own
admission, he had "nowhere to lay his head." We had hoped that he
would be the one to save us. So his death is very sad news for us.

MACNEIL: Thank you, Ms. Rebecca. The studio will provide you with a
Freedom from Arrest Pass so that you can leave safely.

And now, Mr. Bartholomew. . . . Mr. Bartholomew, can you hear me?
Good. As we pointed out earlier, Mr. Bartholomew, who was one of
Joshua's followers, is participating in this program at great personal risk.
First off, Mr. Bartholomew, why are you willing to run that risk?

BARTHOLOMEW: I won't pretend I'm not scared, but after seeing our leader
take risks himself all week, I could hardly call myself a follower of his if I
weren't willing to do the same.

MACNEIL: I see. Were you surprised by the outcome of events this week?

BARTHOLOMEW: Yes, I *was* surprised in the sense that we all hoped we would gain new followers in Jerusalem. But no, I *wasn't* surprised in the sense that his teachings are hard to live out, and people would have to choose for him or against him. You could say that he left no middle ground. You were either for or against.

MACNEIL: Can you describe some of his teachings for our listeners?

BARTHOLOMEW: Mainly it all came down to the need for us to love one another. That sounds a little namby-pamby when you just say it, but as all of us discovered, it's not easy to *do* it. For instance, I don't feel much love right now for Judas, or for Herod and Pilate for that matter. And I doubt General Goliath and I would get along very well. But we have to try, and Joshua promised that if we kept on trying, God would give us power to do a better job at it. He wanted people to work together with each other instead of competing against each other. And he had a big new program people didn't understand very well yet, called the Jubilee Movement, that he had laid out back in Nazareth—that time they tried to shove him over the cliff. It meant sharing our goods, freeing our slaves if we had any, canceling our debts that people owed us—things like that.

MACNEIL: I can understand that certain people might have *wanted* to shove him over the cliff.

BARTHOLOMEW: Yes, but he felt that everyone could change and be part of the Jubilee Movement. He called it conversion, you know, starting all over again. He really believed that everybody—rich, poor, men, women, children, elderly, straight, gay, black, brown, yellow, white—all could be part of a new sort of family.

MACNEIL: It must be disheartening to you to see his program fail.

BARTHOLOMEW: That was my feeling too, when I first looked up at that corpse on the cross just a few hours ago. But there are two things that give me hope that his program won't fail. First of all, there's us, the rest of his group. We may be in hiding right this minute, but pretty soon we'll get our act together, and we'll emerge again, and whatever Joshua stood for, we'll try to stand for, just like he did.

MACNEIL: You said there was a second thing that gave you hope.

BARTHOLOMEW: Yes. I've been thinking over all the things he said. And there's one thing all of us had heard but either forgot or overlooked or couldn't really take seriously. He said that if he died, God would raise him from the dead, surely in the hearts of his people and maybe in some other ways as well.

MACNEIL: Do you believe that?

BARTHOLOMEW: I can't help believing he might be right, and I'm sure that whatever happens, his story won't have ended at three o'clock this afternoon.

MACNEIL: Well, I'm sorry, but our time is up. Thank you, General Goliath, Ms. Rebecca, both here with us in the studio; and Mr. Bartholomew, wherever you are. If you're right, Mr. Bartholomew, that we haven't heard the end of the story of Joshua bar Josef, we'll certainly have to pursue that further on another program. For now, we'll have to wait and see.

I'm Robert MacNeil. Thank you, and good night.

– 14 –

The Life and Times
of Old Tom Didymus (Easter)

Reading: John 20:24–29
Text: Because you have seen me you have found faith. Happy are
they who find faith without seeing me.—John 20:29

In the first part of chapter 20 of the Gospel of John the author tells about various things that happened Easter Sunday morning. He then describes a meeting on Easter Sunday *evening,* in which the disciples, numb with fear, gather behind locked doors. To their surprise, Jesus is suddenly with them, shows them the wounds in his hands and side, blesses them, and breathes the power of the Holy Spirit on them. John continues:

> But one of the Twelve, Thomas the Twin, was not with the rest of them when Jesus came. So the others kept telling him, "We have seen the Lord." But he said, "Unless I see the mark of the nails on his hands, unless I put my finger into the place where the nails were, and my hand into his side, I will never believe it."
> A week later his disciples were once again in the room, and [this time] Thomas was with them. Although the doors were locked, Jesus came and stood among them, saying, "Peace be with you!" Then he said to Thomas, "Reach your finger here; look at my hands. Reach your hand here and put it into my side. Be unbelieving no longer, but believe." Thomas said, "My Lord and my God!" Jesus said to him, "Because you have seen me you have found faith. Happy are they who find faith without seeing me." (John 20:24–29)

I still think it was a good question. We were all together having supper—what actually turned out to be our last supper together—and the Leader was making a long after-dinner speech. Johann was taking notes fast and furiously, and I checked the whole thing out with him later on to be sure I had it right. Anyhow, the Leader is really into a long spiel: the movement is running into hardball opposition, and there are even intimations that a sting operation is under way involving one of our own number, so things around the dinner table are edgy to say the least, everyone wondering if the fellow sitting next to him is a double agent.

Anyhow, the Leader makes clear that we may not even make it through the next twenty-four hours, and that we've got to be prepared for anything. Getting a little poetic (as it seemed to me), he says he'll go to prepare a place for us, and then he'll come back for us, so that we can all be together with him. He puts it, "You know the way I am taking." And that's when I blew my stack, even though the speech was far from over. He had me totally confused, so I just blurted out, "Look, we *don't* know where you are going, so how can we know the way?"

Like I say, I think it was a good question, and I was waiting for a good answer. I didn't get one. In fact, in Johann's notes I emerge as nothing more than a straight man for the Leader, lobbing him an easy question with an easy answer: "You don't know the way?" he asks, surprised-like, and then answers cryptically, "I am the way" along with more stuff about being the truth and the life as well.

Peter and Philip and the other Judas—not the one who turned out to be the double agent—also interrupted along the way, so I wasn't the only one. But they didn't get much satisfaction either. And as sure as my name is Thomas, I think we all left the dining room that evening more confused than when we went in.

It was a wild evening as you may remember, ending up with Judas the double agent tipping off the soldiers that we were all going to the Mount of Olives. And first thing we know they have the Leader in chains, while the rest of us slip out into the darkness as quick as we can, so they won't get chains on us as well.

I

For some very obvious reasons, I stayed in hiding until early the next week. We had a couple of safe houses in Jerusalem where I felt pretty secure, even though I knew the soldiers would be trying to round us all up. Peter showed up on Saturday, either drunk or totally exhausted, with a lot of incoherent muttering about roosters that I couldn't unravel. He's taking it very hard and left almost as soon as he arrived.

Then Andrew and Philip and a couple of others turned up, but they didn't have long faces at all, which surprised me, because from all the reports I'd gotten over the shortwave radio, it was clear that the Leader had been crucified and was as dead as they come, and that without him the movement itself was disintegrating before our eyes.

But the followers had a very different story. Sunday night, they reported, they were hiding in the other safe house with all the doors double-locked, just to be on the safe side, when who should appear in their midst but the Leader! There were no after-dinner speeches this time, but he did show them the nail prints in his hands—so they *told* me—and the spear wound in his side, and then he breathed into them a strange kind of power that took their fear and made them bold, even a bit on the reckless side, as it seemed to me. Substance of their report: the Leader is still alive, or as they were careful to put it, is alive *again,* a distinction that seemed pretty important to them but was too subtle for me.

I simply refused to be taken in. It sounded a mighty unlikely tale, and on top of that I was more than a little ticked off that they had had this big palaver on Sunday night without anybody coming around to see that I was included. But all that aside, it was clear to me that they had been the victims of a collective hallucination, and that they were overcompensating for the death of the Leader by refusing to acknowledge the most elemental fact of human existence (proven to the hilt without exception ever since old man Adam kicked the bucket), namely, that the dead stay dead, the Leader being no exception.

Well, after I had heard just once too often, "We have seen the Leader and he is alive and well," and had been invited to join in the chorus myself, I determined to take a hard line. No reality denial for old Tom. So I laid it flat out, "Unless I see the mark of the nails on his hands, unless I put my finger into the place where the nails were, and my hand into his side [where the spear went], I will never believe it."

I wanted proof—solid, substantial proof. And I wasn't about to settle for anything less. I wasn't the most popular person in the room.

II

He called my bluff, the Leader did. Since we followers hadn't really gotten our act together yet, we all met the *next* Sunday night in another safe house—all except Judas the double agent, of course, who had killed himself when he saw what his betrayal had done. And this time, you may be sure, I was part of the group. There was going to be no more backstage hanky-panky, about which I would be forced to believe somebody else's word. The curtain was going to be all the way up this time.

And then, all of a sudden, there was the Leader again, or at least (to my skeptical eye) somebody who looked like the Leader. After a "Peace be with you" to the whole crowd, he made a beeline for me and said, "Thomas, reach your finger here; look at my hands. Reach your hand here and put it into my side. Be unbelieving no longer, but believe."

Well, that took me off guard, as you might say. If the Leader was alive, I'd have expected him to give me a hard time for not believing what the other members of the movement had told me. But then, I thought, the Leader has always been fair—overdemanding sometimes and stern sometimes, but always fair. I thought about how anybody other than the Leader might just have shoved me in a corner and said, "Who do you think *you* are to get special treatment?" and made me cower. But not the Leader. I was getting the same treatment as all the others had gotten a week earlier. That's the way he operated.

So I suddenly realized, My God, this *is* the Leader, not some phony look-alike trying to take advantage of our grief. So I knelt down and said, "My Lord [my *Kyrios,* as we put it] and my God, you are the one to whom I pledge my loyalty, greater loyalty than to Caesar or anyone else." (Not an idle promise, I might add, being deep in Caesar's territory as we were, and who knew for sure whether the room was bugged or not? And then the Leader, making a teaching occasion out of it, looked at me and said, "Because you have seen me you have found faith. Happy are they who find faith without seeing me."

So pretty soon the spotlight was off old Tom, which I didn't mind at all, since I was beginning to feel a little foolish kneeling there in the midst of a group of grown men. I got up, and the Leader embraced me, and so did all the followers, and I no longer felt like the new kid on the block.

It was all so sudden that later on I checked it out with Johann, always the one with pencil and paper on the ready, and that's pretty much how he had described it. And a lucky thing it was he'd been there, because I needed to check out for sure the last part of what the Leader had said. It's funny, but the thing he didn't say directly to *me* is what I think was most important, and I've never stopped thinking about it: "Happy are they who find faith *without* seeing me."

That soon became an inevitable condition of the future of the movement. Those of us who got in on the ground floor, so to speak, living with the Leader, eating with him, praying with him, sometimes even healing *through* him, had the incredible advantage of having known him face to face, and that clearly wasn't going to continue indefinitely. In fact, what we called the appearances became less and less frequent, and finally stopped altogether.

When you get right down to it, this wasn't really a loss but a gain, since his presence could now be experienced in new ways everywhere—especially where we shared a meal of bread and wine, or we preached about him or (and this was the hardest) tried to live like him. The condition for entering the movement no longer had anything to do with "proofs" like I finally got. It became a matter of people hearing the story and responding for their own reasons—its inner compellingness, or its moral authority, or its ability to empower.

I'm still glad, however, that I went through that terrible time of real doubt, and I mean "real doubt," because I had to learn that assurances don't come *before* an act of faith. People now have to say, "I'll believe without sure proof," and discover that the assurances come only *after* the act of faith. When I went to India, for example, to take the story of the Leader and the movement there, the people there didn't have easy access to faith. They had finally to say, after their own times of doubt, "We'll believe on the basis of your story about the Leader or the kind of life you lead." When they did that (how can I say this?), the story vindicated itself; it was a gateway into further understanding and commitment. And every time we had a convert (and converts were few and far between at first), I'd remember the Leader's words: "Happy are they who find faith without seeing me." Furthermore . . .

[*Here the manuscript breaks off. But there is a postscript, written in a different hand.*]

Johann referred to my brother as Thomas Didymus, or "Thomas the Twin." I'm the Twin. I never got involved in the movement my brother joined, or with the Leader he followed. But after his death, the manuscript you have been reading was brought back from India by one of the followers, who tracked me down and gave it to me. That led me to track down Johann and see what else he had on file about my brother. In terms of bulk it was disappointing, for except for the name Thomas being included in a list of followers, there was only one other reference to him on Johann's whole scroll. But when I read it, lots of questions about my brother's (as I saw it) strange behavior dropped away, and I understood him much better. Here's the story:

Just a few days before the events Johann describes, the followers were on their way to Jerusalem, which anybody who knew anything about anything realized was enemy territory, and that inevitably there would be some serious confrontations. Near Bethany, which is uncomfortably close to Jerusalem, they learned that a close friend named Lazarus had died four days earlier. That's a whole story in itself that I can't recount here. But the upshot of this news was that the Leader felt that even though going to comfort Lazarus's sisters would be a dangerous operation, and politically inopportune, to say the least, they ought to do it anyway. "Lazarus is dead," the Leader said, and then (a little inconsistently, it always has seemed to me) "let us go to him."

That's not what you might call a popular proposal, especially when every tree or bush or rock might be hiding some of Herod's militia, and there was a deafening silence when the Leader dropped that particular conversational bombshell. But listen to what comes next. Johann records that "Thomas, called 'The Twin,' said to his fellow followers, 'Let us also go and die with him.' " Whether that just slipped out before he could control it, or was sheer bravado, or was straight from the heart, I count that as the high point of my brother's life. Yes, he also said all those other things about not knowing the way, and demanding sure and certain "proof." But when it was payoff time, when the followers had to fish or cut bait, when they had to act without proof ahead of time that they would even live to tell the tale—that's when Thomas displayed his true colors. The Leader is in a tough spot, and needs support, and even so may not escape with his life? "Okay," says Tom, "let us also go and die with him."

And you know something? He finally got his wish. For when the follower from India found me and gave me the mementos of my brother's life, he also told me that there had been people in India who didn't like his message, and that they had shown their displeasure by inflicting on him a martyr's death.

O God, you give us many examples by whom to test the integrity of our faith, and by whom to be empowered in the living of that faith. Encourage in us a healthy doubt and skepticism that is the absolute precursor of a tested faith, and empower us on the far side of your questions and concerns to live as the followers of the Leader you sent.

We know we are not likely to be martyrs in the usual sense, but we remember that a martyr is a witness, whether in life or in death. So help us to be witnesses to you in the way we live, and even, if occasion demands it, in the way we die. In the name of the Leader, Jesus Christ, we pray. Amen.

The Apocryphal Council
of Alexandria
(Trinity Sunday)

Reading: 2 Corinthians 13:13

Text: The grace of the Lord Jesus Christ, and the love of God, and fellowship in the Holy Spirit, be with you all.—2 Corinthians 13:13

In a gallery in Paris there hangs a rather well known painting. If one asks what the subject of the painting is, one gets the answer, "That's a pipe." But the artist is ready for this response and has already given the painting a title: *Ceci n'est pas un pipe* (This is not a pipe). And the artist has the last laugh. Clearly it is not a pipe; try smoking it and discover how unsatisfactory this two-dimensional object is as a pipe. The artist's defense, if pressed, is to reiterate that it is *not* a pipe, it is only a *picture* of a pipe.

It may seem a long way from that insight to an Apocryphal Early Church Council trying to define a doctrine of the Trinity. But there is an interesting overlap. For too often in church history attempts have been made to offer statements that purport to tell us exactly who God is, the doctrine of the Trinity being a frequent case in point. Attached to every such attempt should be a title reading something like "Ceci n'est pas Dieu" (This is not God). If pressed, the dogmatician should have the same recourse the artist had: to restate that the doctrine is not God, it is a picture, or an image, or a formulation, or a concept about God, *and no more than that.*

This is why it makes sense to recognize that there is no "doctrine of the Trinity" in the Bible. There are, however, many experiences of the presence and reality of God in the Bible, which, when attempts were made to describe them, yielded language and images that with amazing consistency contained three interrelated kinds of assertions about God. The clearest examples of this phenomenon at work are in the benedictions with which some early Christians often concluded their liturgies or their letters. The clearest single example is the ending of 2 Corinthians, where Paul writes, "The grace of the Lord Jesus Christ, and the love of God, and fellowship in the Holy Spirit be with you all."

Christians, then, do not place their faith in "the doctrine of the Trinity," an intellectual formulation that may or may not prove helpful in describing belief about God. Christians do believe in the God toward whom the Trinitarian formulations point. The difference is crucial. Keeping that difference alive is all that the Apocryphal Council of Alexandria can expect to achieve. The document comprises the minutes of this early church council that got lost in the sands of Egypt during a purge of heretics and have only recently been rediscovered.

TITUS (*who is obviously finishing up a long speech*): . . . So we've got to come clean on what we really mean by "God," or we will lose the young people, already being attracted to Egyptian animal worship. They want some straight answers.

ANDRONICUS: I'm all for that. And besides, if we're going to be thrown to the lions anyway, we at least ought to be able to say why. For starters, esteemed chairman—since the only images that can communicate either to the young people or to the lion tamers are drawn from our own experience—I want to emphasize the power and wonder and creativity and love of God that we inherited from the Hebrews. And when I try to find an image for that, of a God who really loves us and woos us and cares for us (and, when necessary, chastises us) well, the best image I can think of is one who "mothers" us as well.

TITUS (*after some hesitation*): I don't know whether that last image of yours, Andronicus, will fly in Alexandria, let alone Byzantium. Perhaps we should put it on hold for now, or try it out unofficially for a while, and then conduct a few polls. Furthermore, as I consider the gender ratio at this particular council, I think we would have considerably better chances of success if we settle for "father" as a primary image. Same idea, of course, as "mother," but less unsettling. (*musing*) "Parent" would also work, but it doesn't scan as well in Greek.

ANDRONICUS: I think you're too timid. Whether we say mother or father or parent, the basic message is that God is personal and cares for us. An image like creator ought to be in there as well, since we human beings create out of love and tend to love what we create. That surely goes for God as well.

FLAVIUS: That's all okay for openers, but we haven't yet touched on our *distinctive* message to the whole Empire. The folks out there know about a God who creates and loves and woos, because they've been persecuting the Jews for centuries, and some of that Jewish belief has rubbed off on them. But we've got to give central place to that fact that that same God really lived among us not so long ago, and looked much like us. *True God* in our midst, that's the message. Messiah, Liberator, Logos—there are dozens of ways to say it.

SIXTUS: Now wait a minute! That's too restrictive. When we talk about "God in our midst" (and I assume it is Joshua bar Josef of Galilee to whom you are referring), you've only given half the message. We'd better make clear that this Joshua bar Joseph not only shows us who God is but also shows us who we are—or rather, who we are meant to be. So he is not only true God but *true humanity* as well—comforter, friend, judge, hope.

TITUS (*uneasily*): Sixtus, it appears that you and Flavius are working at cross-purposes. Either Joshua bar Josef was truly God or he was truly human. You can't have it both ways. Oil and water, you know.

FLAVIUS AND SIXTUS (*simultaneously, each one fearful of being upstaged by the other*): I move we put it to a vote.

TITUS: Very well. Those who favor "true God" raise their hands. . . . Sixty-two. Now, those who favor "true humanity" raise their hands. . . . H'mm. Sixty-two. It's a tie. (*pensively*) The council did not give me the power to break a tie.

FLAVIUS AND SIXTUS (*simultaneously*): Let us retain both emphases.

SIXTUS: Either statement by itself is inadequate.

FLAVIUS: Affirming both together will at least remind people that we approach the meaning of Joshua bar Josef in different ways, and that no one way has all the truth. And we need to remember that later followers of the Way may find new images we haven't even thought of.

TITUS: You are granting a lot of power to the future, Flavius, but since we are talking about a "living God," it's probably appropriate not to carve our own notions too indelibly in stone. Well, this may provide a satisfactory outcome to our deliberations. Do I hear a motion to adjourn?

CRITO (*interrupting*): Point of order, point of order! The chair wrongly assumes that we have said all we have to say. Even though Andronicus and Flavius have described how God is real for *them,* I must add something more. We are not talking just about a God from the past but (as your last comment reminded us, esteemed Titus) of a God who is active in the *present,* the same God we have been talking about in other terms all afternoon, indeed throughout the whole of this council.

TITUS: Come to the point, Crito. How would you describe *this* aspect of God?

CRITO: Like my distinguished predecessors, all I've got to offer are images, but I remind you that they are our crucial resource. God's living presence today? It's like the rush of a mighty wind, like the power of breathing, like the cleansing of fire or water, like a Spirit moving over and under and within our lives. (*He is getting quite worked up.*) This Spirit gives me access to Joshua bar Josef, just as Joshua bar Josef gives me access to the Creator who loves us—Father or Mother or Parent or whatever term we decided upon earlier.

TITUS (*who is often hovering on the brink of heresy*): I take it, then, Crito, that you are urging this council to define not two, but *three* Gods?

CRITO (*still worked up*): Oh no, no, no, not at all. *Not* three Gods! *One* God, whom we know in three different ways, each of which conjures up a multitude of images. The images will never be sufficient. They can only be pointers, human pointers, but they're the best we've got for right now.

TITUS: Thank you for straightening me out, Crito. As a result of all of these contributions, I will rule that the proceedings of this council register a belief (a) that there is *one* God, (b) that we are confronted by this God in three basic ways, (c) that our struggle to find adequate images for that confrontation is a never-ending one, and (d) that subsequent councils should continue these explorations. I trust the secretary has that all down.

To conclude, I state as my own opinion that while many councils will deal with this or that specific heresy in the future, the greatest heresy will be any attempt to stifle the search for fresh images for God appropriate to the culture in which they originate. No council will ever say the last word.

TITUS, ANDRONICUS, FLAVIUS, CRITO: Move to adjourn.

Part 3
Confronting a World

There's a world out there. It is not alien territory for Christians. It is where Christians belong, precisely because it is where Jesus Christ chose to belong. As a consequence, Christianity is firmly lodged in the midst of the earthy, the earthly, the historical, the sensual, the human. Not somewhere else. Sermons must make a connection between the biblical story and our everyday contemporary stories and urge that they are part of a single overarching story. Karl Barth, a Swiss theologian, put it best, "The Christian must always read with the Bible in one hand and the morning newspaper in the other." In the following chapters some crises are confronted: hatred, political prisoners, violence, racism, sexuality and homosexuality, war, taxes. What do we *say* about them? What do we *do* about them? How does the Bible help us in the saying and the doing? If some of the references seem "dated," reflect on the fact that nothing has changed except the names and locations of the participants.

– 16 –

"How Shall We Sing
the Lord's Song
in a Strange Land?"

Reading: Psalm 137, *in toto*.

The psalmist and the psalmist's people are in exile. Their land of Zion has been invaded and they have been carted off to the land of the Babylonians who (with help from the Edomites) have sacked and destroyed the sacred city of Jerusalem. The Israelites are enemy aliens, outsiders, prisoners of war, who do not feel at home in their strange new location and who (to make things worse) are being taunted by their captors. In the face of all this, the psalmist works up a rousing appeal to them to keep alive the memory of the earlier days in Jerusalem.

So ends the prescribed lectionary reading at the end of verse 6.

Almost nobody ever reads the three final verses of the psalm for reasons that will be apparent when I break with liturgical custom and do so this morning. I do so because their vindictive flavor illustrates a further problem with which we have to cope today.

> By the rivers of Babylon we sat down and wept,
> as we remembered Zion.
> On the willow trees there
> we hung our harps,
> for there those who had carried us captive
> asked us to sing a song.
> Our captors called on us to be joyful:
> "Sing us one of the songs of Zion!"
> How shall we sing the Lord's song
> in a strange land?
> If I forget you, Jerusalem,
> may my right hand wither away;
> let my tongue cling to the roof of my mouth
> if I do not remember you,
> if I do not set Jerusalem
> above my chief joy.

Remember, Lord, against the Edomites
the day when Jerusalem fell,
how they shouted, "Down with it, down with it,
down to its very foundations!"
Babylon, Babylon, the destroyer,
happy is the one who repays you
for what you did to us!
Happy is the one who seizes your little ones
and dashes them against a rock!

It's not uncommon to feel that we are dwelling in "a strange land." It happens every time we move to a new location, start a new job, enroll in a new school, or travel for the first time to a foreign country. We are not just strangers, but outsiders—those who don't belong, those who don't get the "in" jokes, those who are baffled by knowing glances that go right past us. Perhaps the strongest expression of this is to feel like aliens, literally foreigners, people who belong to a different nationality, race, or culture—misfits.

The scripture reading is a classic instance of being all of the above—strangers, outsiders, foreigners, misfits. We empathize with the Israelites because we share a sense of their discomfort. We would love to see them freed up, because that might give *us* some pointers on how to escape being outsiders, strangers, misfits.

I

If that is our hope, then the first message of the biblical story as a whole can only be disconcerting. For it clearly tells us that we are *called* to be strangers and misfits, those who in the well-known image of Henry David Thoreau, "march to the beat of a different drummer," and are thus out of step with the crowd. Cardinal Suhard, archbishop of Paris during the Nazi occupation, wrote to his parishioners, "[To be a witness] means living in such a way that one's life would make no sense if God did not exist."

A biblical account of this role is found in the eleventh chapter of Hebrews, where the author repeatedly describes the people of God as being on a *journey*, always finding themselves in new and different locations, "strangers and exiles on the earth" as the writer puts it, those who have not "arrived," but are always on the march, seeking a homeland, or as the author puts it, "a city that has foundations, whose builder and maker is God."

Now that's a pretty comprehensive recipe for being a stranger, an outsider, but it's also a pretty inclusive description of being a Christian. However, there is a fine line to walk here, and ordinary Christians like ourselves fall off one side or the other with predictable regularity. We miss the point if we say, on the one hand, "Let's keep our sights focused exclusively on heaven or some alternate vision and scorn the earth." That makes us irrelevant and finally ungrateful for all the possibilities God gives us. But we miss the point equally, if we say, on the other hand, "Let's focus exclusively on the here and now, and forget any visions or the beat of different drummers." That makes us uncritical and finally implicates us in evil, since we have no vantage point from which to judge it or oppose it.

The Christian stance is always a matter of giving a *provisional* loyalty to the claims of the "strange land," but never a *final* loyalty. And the way we keep those two loyalties related to one another is precisely to "sing the Lord's song" (not somebody else's song) and to sing it right in the midst of the "strange land" (not somewhere else). It will be a different song from the other songs that are being sung, and that will represent its contribution to the strange land.

II

So there's nothing new about the claim that Christians live in a strange land, or the claim that Christians are called to sing the Lord's song within it. That has always gone with the territory. What needs to be emphasized is that such a role has never been more important than right now, when all we are hearing, in the aftermath of the Gulf War, are victory songs, and the temptation to self-delusion is almost overpowering.

Since the war ended, we have entered into a strange new land we need to examine, in order to know what the content of the Lord's song should be, for if people like us do not sing *that* song, I am afraid no one else will. The issue is no longer whether it would be right or wrong to go to war. That chapter in our lives has been written: we went to war. The question is: What do we do and say now, whether we supported going to war or not? Can we find a message to share?

Like the people in the psalm, perhaps our first reaction should be to *weep* (v. 1) at all the devastation, all the death, precisely at the moment when everybody else is cheering. Like the people in the psalm, perhaps our second reaction should be to retreat into *reflective silence* (v. 4), precisely at the moment when everybody else is so exuberantly shouting. Like the people in the psalm, perhaps our third reaction should be one of personal *devastation* (v. 3) as we reflect tremulously on the question they initially asked in near despair, "How *shall* we sing the Lord's song in a strange land?" knowing that if we try to sing it, we also may be jeered at, just as they were.

The thing that saved them, and can save us, is that in the midst of exile they appealed finally to *memory* (vv. 5–6), "If I forget you, Jerusalem, may my right hand wither away; let my tongue cling to the roof of my mouth." They remembered their past as Jews. We must remember our past as Christians: remember the way the midwives in the exodus story stood up to Pharaoh in the name of freedom for the slaves; remember the way the prophets "spoke truth to power" against foreign rulers and their own rulers; remember the way Jesus stood up to Herod and Pilate and said "no" to both of them; remember the way St. Francis stood up to the Saracens, pleading for peace; remember the way Martin Luther stood up to both king and pope in the name of truth; remember the way Martin Luther King, Jr., stood up against racists and witnessed to the power of love; remember the way the martyred Roman Catholic sisters stood up to the corrupt Salvadoran government, knowing how costly it would be to do so. They all sang the Lord's song in a strange land, and they were *misfits,* every one of them.

Why does this land, in the aftermath of war, seem so strange and so frightening? I can only tell you what I see, hoping that you see some of the things I do:

I see a nation hysterically happy and proud—appropriately *happy* that most of our loved ones are returning unharmed, but inappropriately *proud* that we killed tens of thousands of strange people called Arabs, and they killed almost none of us. Three cheers for our side.

I see a nation glorying in the sheer power of military might, chanting the claim that we are number one again and intend to stay that way.

I see a people overjoyed that we rushed in and played the bully when we might at least have thought twice and tried to play the diplomat.

I see a people who are exultant that we have demonstrated that we can go anywhere in the world we wish—whether it be Grenada, Panama, or Kuwait—and impose our will on tiny nations by sheer force of arms.

I see legislators already proclaiming that anyone who ever had any doubts about the absolute rightness of Operation Desert Storm is unfit to hold public office, a charge we are going to hear incessantly through the 1992 campaign.

I see the Commander in Chief of the Armed Forces (who also lives in the White House) proclaiming without a whisper of self-doubt that God blessed our efforts in a *totally* just war where all the wrong was on their side and all the right was on ours.

I see a people saying, "We needed this war to make us feel good about ourselves again!"—without a pause to reflect that the cost of making us "feel good about ourselves" was the blood of tens of thousands of Iraqis, whom we had never met and with whom even our President conceded we had no quarrel.

I see a nation persuading itself that war has now become scientific and impersonal, a sanitized three-dimensional Nintendo game, from which mangled bodies and screaming children and weeping mothers have somehow been eliminated—even when we know that's not the way it is, and that it only *looks* that way because we have been taken in by the military censors who controlled the media.

It is not a strange land because many evil things have happened—that is the stuff of all human history. It is a strange land *because we cheer what has happened*—91 percent of us, according to the polls. What is so frightening is that no one seems to feel any qualms. No one is asking: Was it worth the toll in human lives? Was it worth the destruction of two countries? Was it worth the hatred we will reap from the Arab world? Was it worth setting a precedent that will be so easy to repeat a second time, and a third time, at some other trouble spot in the world? Was it worth it to get better access to oil?

It is *that* situation into which we have to try to insert the Lord's song. There are some things to cheer: that the war was short, that poison gas was not used, that our young men and women are already returning home. But the voices of Christians are not needed to swell the throngs of the cheerleaders. Ninety-one percent of the population is doing an efficient job at that. The voices of Christians—9 percent of the population—are needed to say the things no one else is saying, to ask the questions no one else is asking. Along with the paeans of joy, there must also be pleas for forgiveness, pleas for empowerment to draw some good out of great evil, a willingness to acknowledge that war is the worst possible way to resolve human conflicts, and that its use represents a failure within the human family for which we need to repent.

I believe that we will get our best clues for how to do such things not from the winners but from the losers, among whom I cannot but believe that God is present in special and comforting ways: lavishing attention not only on the fliers of the ten thousand bombing sorties, but even more on those who were on the receiving end of the bombs: close not only to joyful families appropriately grateful to God that their sons and daughters are returning unharmed, but even closer to the eighty-seven U.S. families who will receive only corpses as the troops come home; and closer yet to the thousands and thousands of Iraqi and Kuwaiti families who face only a grim and devastating future. Let us remember those families as well; let us try to see the war through their eyes, to feel their pain, to face their kind of future. And then perhaps new words for the Lord's song will come to us.

III

It is tempting to stop there. We would have been faithful to the lectionary's decision to include only the first six verses of the psalm, and, as an added bonus, the sermon would have been six minutes shorter than usual.

But we must also hear those final harsh words in verses 7–9, which remind us bluntly and brutally that *memory is a two-edged sword.* It makes all the difference *what* we remember, and the *use* to which we put those memories. The psalmist, after a noble evocation of the memory of Jerusalem, goes utterly berserk and uses the memory to fuel revenge: "We will pay you back, you Babylonians and Edomites. Someday we will round up your kids and bash their brains out at the nearest rock pile." That's a very human reaction, when you have seen your entire universe crumble, but it is not to be confused with the Word of God.

Nobody's talking that way right now, and revenge is not high on people's agendas. But revenge is very easy to cultivate, and there are already telltale signs of the beginning of revenge, to which attention must be paid before they have a chance to become festering wounds, and lead us down the path the psalmist walked.

A typical telltale sign is a casual remark made by the President on the day of victory. The President deserves commendation at least for insisting throughout the struggle that we had no quarrel with the Iraqi people, but only with Saddam Hussein. But on the day of victory, he said that he wanted to be sure that "not one American dime" would go toward the rebuilding of Iraq.

That is a total reversal of his earlier high ground in distinguishing between the Iraqi people and their leader. If not one American dime goes toward the rebuilding of an Iraq we have pulverized, it is the Iraqi *people* who will suffer, not their leader, and our nation will be saying that we *do* have a quarrel with the Iraqi people. Pushed logically, the position becomes: "Your hospitals are destroyed? Tough. Your schools and homes are in rubble? Dig your way out, stone by stone. Your bridges are gone? Learn to swim. Your civilians are dead? Let their corpses putrefy. You dug your hole, now lie in it."

I am not attributing such attitudes to the President and others who prosecuted the war, but I am saying that such attitudes grow rapidly in our minds, just as they grew rapidly in the mind of the psalmist. We have an unequivocal duty to challenge them. It will not do to repudiate revenge in wartime only to affirm it in peacetime.

The content of the Lord's song is increasingly clear: we may not use memory as an instrument of vengeance; we are not permitted to use memory to draw, from our own past, attitudes that are destructive and mean-spirited; we must draw from our own past those things that are creative and noble. And then we can use this recent national experience to begin to build a world in which none of the events of the past weeks will ever have to be repeated again.

O God, it would be much more convenient for us if you hadn't told us that all people are equally your children, and that the part of your message about loving includes loving enemies as well as friends. But since you appear unwilling to change the ground rules, help us to get a new sense of what they might mean in our own day, so that we can begin to sing your song in ways that might even attract other people to join in the chorus. In Jesus' name. Amen.

– 17 –

The Spiral of Violence

Reading: Amos 5:14–15, 21–24

About 750 B.C., a country boy named Amos emerges from a sycamore grove and goes to the big city of Bethel to bring the charges of God's judgment against Judah. But he also offers advice and hope to a remnant that was hanging in there, as the first part of the lesson indicates:

> Seek good and not evil
> that you may live,
> that God, the God of hosts,
> may be with you,
> as you claim.
> Hate evil and love good;
> establish justice in the courts.
> It may be that God, the God of hosts,
> will show favor to the
> remnant of Joseph.
>
> (Amos 5:14–15)

And then, more militantly, God speaks to the "religious" folk. I have changed these verses only by offering contemporary counterparts for things like "grain-offerings" and the offerings of "the flesh of stall-fed beasts," which are not part of the ongoing life of most of us. God speaks:

> I spurn with loathing
> your offering,
> I take no pleasure
> in your liturgies.
> Spare me the sound of your hymn singing,
> I will not even listen to your brand-new pipe organ—
> unless
> along with them
> justice flows down like waters
> and righteousness like a mighty stream.
>
> (Amos 5:21–24)

During the Vietnam years, William Sloane Coffin, then chaplain of Yale University, was able to get an appointment with a few other ministers to meet with the Secretary of State, Henry Kissinger. The exchange grew rather heated, and finally, in exasperation, Kissinger said to Coffin, "All right, how would *you* get the boys home from Vietnam?" Bill Coffin, never one to leave a question unanswered, responded, "Mr. Kissinger, our job is to proclaim that justice must roll down like waters, and righteousness like a mighty stream. Your job, Mr. Kissinger, is to work out the details of the irrigation system."

I have neither the intention nor the competence to come up with a re-designed irrigation system for America, after the fires of Los Angeles less than two weeks ago. I do, however, propose to comment on some of the perspectives we must bring to bear on a task that has become so much more urgent after the last dozen days.

I

First of all, how are we to interpret the riots after the Rodney King verdict? The prevailing viewpoint goes something like this: "There was a terrible outbreak of violence last week. A bunch of hoods and hoodlums ran amok and gave America a bad name both at home and abroad. It was an ugly parenthesis in the life of our nation. But it's now time to rebuild and get back to the way things were before the riots."

What I say this morning is predicated on the opposite conviction—that the last dozen days were not just an ugly blip on the screen of our national life, but are already *a defining moment* for us and our nation. They have shown us at least two things about our society that we did not want to see. One of these is the pervasive presence of *racism* (witness the verdict in the trial of the four Los Angeles cops), and the other is the pervasive presence of *violence* (witness the aftermath of the verdict). We have learned that we are a racist society and a violent society.

We have a word in our Christian vocabulary for "a defining moment," and we need to bring it center stage. It is the Greek word *kairos*. It is used in contrast to another Greek word, *chronos,* from which we get words like "chronology" and "chronometer." *Chronos,* in other words, is clock time, ordinary measurable time—the succession of seconds, minutes, hours, days, weeks, months, years, centuries, aeons, about which we can do precisely nothing.

That wasn't good enough for the early Christians, who used the word *kairos* instead of *chronos* when they wanted to describe a *special* time rather than ordinary time—a time full of possibilities for good and for evil, a momentous time that might never come again, a time for decision making. Jesus' first recorded words are the announcement in Mark 1:15 that "the *kairos* has arrived; the kingdom of God has broken in" —obviously far from an ordinary, routine announcement. And the announcement was also an appeal, a demand: "Repent," Jesus goes on (which means "turn around, start over, reverse your course"), "repent and believe the good news."

A *kairos* is a time, then, when new things become clear, when we can no longer close our eyes or stop our ears, and ignore what is going on all around us. The last dozen days have been a *kairos* for us, a special time we cannot ignore—a time calling for change. They have shown us things that have been true for a long time, but that we didn't want to believe. They have shown us a miscarriage of *justice* in the courts—but not the first miscarriage, only one among hundreds, as any member of a minority group can tell us. They have shown us the *violence* of the inner city—but not the first such expression of violence in the inner city, which has been going on for decades and generations—ask any black, Hispanic, Asian, or resident of the inner city. Without condoning the looting and the hooting and the shooting, we must try to understand why the rage spilled forth: the cap had been on the bottle too long, and the incendiary mixture needed only a single event to ignite it.

So it's *kairos* time for us. Whatever were our blindnesses before, the scales have been ripped off our heretofore unseeing eyes.

II

If it is *kairos* time, what tools do we have for understanding it? I offer a tool: an analysis by one of the great Christian leaders of our time, the former archbishop of Recife, Brazil, Dom Helder Câmara. It is what he calls the spiral of violence.

Dom Helder describes three kinds of violence. Violence No. 1 he calls *injustice.* Any violation of personhood is an act of violence, whether physical force is used or not. To deny food to a hungry child is an act of violence. To deny a job to an able-bodied man or woman is an act of violence. To taunt a person for having different skin color is an act of violence. To have a two-tier system of justice—one for Anglos and another for people of color—is an act of violence. To live in a society where these things happen is to live in a violent society.

When the cumulative effects of injustice, Violence No. 1, become too much to bear, there is a *revolt,* which Dom Helder calls Violence No. 2. The victims of cumulative violence finally rise up and say, "Enough!" A small incident sparks a revolt, and the unintended result escalates into a riot, as in Detroit in 1942, in Harlem in 1944, in Watts in 1965, in Los Angeles in 1992, and in dozens of other cities during the intervening years.

And no sooner has Violence No. 2, revolt, begun to irrupt than the power of the state moves in and says, "You can't do this!" and Violence No. 3, *repression,* is imposed. The National Guard is mobilized, or the Marines are sent in, or the army is called up, or maybe all three at once. Whatever repressive measures are necessary to stop the revolt are employed. (A former mayor of Chicago used to talk approvingly about "a warning shot in the stomach.")

The governmental repression leaves things worse than they were before, so the result is *more* injustice than ever, which leads to *more* explosive revolt, which leads to *more* massive repression, which leads to even worse injustice, even worse revolt and even worse repression. And there you have the spiral of violence: injustice, revolt, repression, injustice, revolt, repression—on and on and on.

The question is, How do we break the spiral of violence? The answer our society invariably offers is, You break the spiral the minute Violence No. 2 (revolt) surfaces, when rocks and knives and guns appear and law and order breaks down.

And Dom Helder responds that that always comes too late. The only way finally to break the spiral of violence is to attack it at the level of Violence No. 1, injustice. Anything that does not get to the root of the injustice will only be cosmetic—putting a Band-Aid on a deep wound without even cleaning the wound out.

If all that happens as a result of the last dozen days is that we breathe a collective sigh of relief and make token contributions to rebuilding, we will have guaranteed that the spiral will continue with worse outbursts in the future.

What would it mean to take the spiral of violence seriously? If *injustice* is the problem, the poetic words of Amos that Bill Coffin quoted to Henry Kissinger assume the character of hard-nosed reality: "Let justice roll down like waters, and righteousness like a mighty stream" (Amos 5:24).

We all have ideas about what the priorities ought to be in combating injustice in our society. My own feeling is that the key issues are *education* and *jobs* and that they cannot be separated. Better education is a necessity for any job that is more than menial labor, and we have systematically denied better education to minority groups in the last decades. And that means that in turn we have denied them significant job opportunities. Of course other things are needed as well: affordable housing for the poor, access to health care for all, ways to acquire a feeling of self-worth. But whatever priorities emerge, we as a nation are going to have to deal with these root causes of racial inequality, provide quality education, and jobs in the hundreds of thousands, even in the millions, job programs created by the society, if necessary, until a new economy is geared up for action.

The unpopular thing that we Christians are going to have to say is that any serious attention to the root causes of racism and unemployment is going to be very expensive. And if we really believe that it is no longer business as usual, those of us in the churches—who are supposed to have a deep commitment to alleviating the plight of the neighbor—are going to have to convince people that there is a massive social price tag attached to achieving a just society. That price tag makes the expenditures now being discussed almost laughable in their inadequacy—save that none of the victims are laughing. Halfway measures will be worse than nothing, for they will simply say to minority groups that we don't really care enough to want to make a difference. And if we are not willing to do that, our words are going to be full of sound and fury, and in this case signifying *less* than nothing.

So welcome, sisters and brothers, to an unappealing but absolutely essential crusade for higher taxes as well as lower expenditures. It will never again be business as usual.

III

It is not enough just to look at the spiral of violence in overall terms. We must also ask what we, as people of faith, can do to respond right here to a *kairos* time that features a spiral of violence. Here is an initial laundry list of items that need expansion and refinement.

Adult study classes in our churches could sponsor sessions on racism and the reasons (which come close to the bone) for its tenacious hold on our culture and our lives.

Groups concerned about "church and society" could establish bridgeheads with churches coming from different racial and ethnic backgrounds.

Worship committees could invite people to share our pulpits who come from those different racial and cultural backgrounds to help challenge prevalent middle-class misunderstandings of the gospel. New liturgies and music could emancipate us from totally western, and therefore provincial, expressions of our faith.

Governing bodies in our churches could examine what the new urgency on issues of racism and violence say to us about our local and national policies, so that we do not return to business as usual.

Membership concerns need to be broadened by active recruitment of members of minority groups, not to provide token integration or make us look better, but because we so desperately need their help in this *kairos* time if we are truly to be "the whole people of God" and not just a pale reflection of our culture. We need to ask minority members to help us see the world through their eyes, since our own angle of vision is too narrow. After urging them to "tell it like it is," we must be willing to listen, especially when the message is uncomfortable.

Sunday school and youth programs need greater racial mixtures than we presently have. It will be the next generation rather than ours that will really model significant breakthroughs, if they come.

Budgetary considerations must start to close the gap between what affluent churches keep for themselves and what they make available for others. This will count for more than all the noble intentions and high-sounding prose coming from this or any other pulpit.

IV

If we take any of this seriously, it boils down to *risk taking,* setting ourselves against the stream, being at odds with the majority, appearing strange to our friends and, in fact, going through the process of reversal called conversion. If that sounds terribly lonely, I offer two bits of good news: (1) risk taking is nothing new; it goes clear back to the Hebrew prophets; and (2) risk taking is not done alone. We not only have that great "cloud of witnesses" in scripture, we have each other, and through each other we have direct access to the power of God. We are not to be loners.

There is a final source of strength: faith is not only *demand,* it is also *promise.* Demand may be the order of the day right now, but Jesus also says some initially strange things about how "my yoke is easy and my burden is light." The heavy burdens turn out to be burdens that are shared within a communion of saints that exists in this very place. We often hear the statement of George Santayana that "those who forget history are doomed to repeat it." I offer a more liberating version: "Those who remember history are empowered to redirect it." That is the exciting challenge of a time of *kairos:* it is not only a time to be sober but a time to take heart.

> Come Lord
> Do not smile and say
> You are already with us.
> Millions do not know you
> and to us who do,
> what is the difference?
> What is the point of your presence
> if our lives do not alter?

Change our lives, shatter
our complacency.
Make your word
flesh of our flesh,
blood of our blood
and our life's purpose.
Take away the quietness
of a clear conscience.
Press us uncomfortably.
For only thus
that other peace is made,
your peace.
Amen.
(Dom Helder Câmara, *The Desert Is Fertile*)

– 18 –

Sexuality and Homosexuality:
A Problem for the Churches

Reading: Genesis 1–2:4a

Few pieces of literature have been subject to more minute examination than the opening chapters of Genesis. Amid much conjecture, a few things seem clear:

1. There are two accounts of the creation story that later editors wove into one.

2. The lectionary account (Gen. 1–2:4a) is the later account chronologically, but the earlier account textually. The last has become first.

3. The passage is not a scientific attempt to answer How questions: How did creation get going? How did life come from nonlife? Instead, the passage is a poetic attempt to answer Why questions: Why a world anyway? Why the sky? Why living creatures? Why sex? The literary form is a *myth,* a story from back then that sheds light on here and now rather than a story that is pretend or make-believe.

4. Myths are important sources of wisdom. Myths can also be abused. In the one we will examine, there is enough interpretive elbowroom for people to claim biblical warrant to exploit creation for their own ends. In the other creation story (Gen. 2:4b-ff.) there are sexist passages that demean women. We must repudiate interpretations like these.

Our authors are *telling a story,* and they invite us to hear it on their terms: the creation of light and darkness, a vault called heaven, water and dry land and vegetation, stars, sun and moon, living creatures (sea monsters and birds) cattle (wild animals and reptiles). The culminating section of the story deals with the final stage of creation, the creation of human beings:

God said, "Let the earth bring forth living creatures, according to their various kinds: cattle, creeping things, and wild animals, all according to their various kinds. So it was; God made wild animals, cattle and every creeping thing, all according to their various kinds; *And God saw that it was good.* Then God said, "Let us make human beings in our image, after our likeness, to

have dominion over the fish of the sea, the birds of the air, the cattle, all wild
animals on land, and everything that creeps on the earth."
   God created human beings in God's own image;
   in the image of God, God created them;
   male and female God created them. . . .
   So it was; and God saw all that God had made, and *it was very good.* (Genesis 1:24–27, 31, italics added)

There are some surprises in this ancient story, which is often seen as repressive, and yet has virtually untapped possibilities for liberation.

I

   The first surprise—the connection between the goodness of God and
the goodness of sex—is not hard to establish. Take this wonderful text
from Genesis, the claim that "God created human beings in God's own image; in the image of God, God created them; male and female God created
them" (Gen. 1:27). This affirmation tells us something about ourselves and
something about God, and the two affirmations go together.
   About ourselves it tells us in the most extravagant terms that we are neither dust nor divinity, but rather that we are unique in the created order.
Our best clue to who God is comes when we look at other persons. We "image" God, we "reflect" God, we are that part of the created order most like
the Creator. We have to be spoken of in the plural. We are not complete
persons as isolated individuals; rather, our individuality, that which makes
us who we uniquely are, is achieved *in relationship.* We are fully human
only when we are part of community. The "image of God" in us is not fully
realized if we point only to Fred here and Mary there. We must point to
Fred and Mary *together,* neither one complete, "whole," or fully a person,
save in reciprocity with one another.
   Surprisingly, this is also what the passage tells us *about God.* God, too,
is only fully understood in terms of relationship—within the godhead we
have what the church has come to call creativity, redeeming love, and
outward-turning empowerment, for which the traditional words have
been Father, Son, and Holy Spirit. There is a sense in which relationship
and intermingling exist within the divine being. And we "image" that
kind of intermingling in our own lives.
   God-in-relationship has another meaning as well: God is most fully
God, not when dwelling alone in isolated splendor, but in relationship . . . with us. That's what it means to talk about love—in this case
God's love, always reaching out to us through creation, through Christ,

and through community—another set of words that point to what Father, Son, and Holy Spirit meant to our theological ancestors. God is always God-in-relationship—and to the degree that we "image" God, we, too, are always in relationship, to one another and to God. Whatever else our ways of speaking about God mean, they surely mean most of all that God, and we, are fully who we are meant to be only through the giving and taking, the reciprocity, that we find in God's outgoing love to us, and in our outgoing love to one another and to God.

The human example of God-in-relationship that the Genesis passage gives us is the example of "male and female," in relationship. (In case you hadn't noticed, that is a very big plug for sex.) The love that is expressed in the sexual relationship, the Bible tells us, is our absolutely best clue not only to the nature of human love but to the nature of divine love as well. "Male and female God created them" and God saw not only that this particular act of creation was "good," but that it was "*very* good."

II

So much is clear in this passage, and we do well to recall it, especially when the media and changing mores are reducing sex to calisthenics and little more. But we must immediately go on to a second surprise in the story, which entails reading it *as a myth,* and not as biology or cultural anthropology. What we learn from Genesis, as we have seen, is that the key in understanding God and ourselves is *relationship*. It is in mutuality, in sharing, that God's love and human love are experienced. The example used in the story is the relationship of "male and female."

But we know, as we reflect on the matter, that this single example does not begin to exhaust the instances of deep and caring relationships among human beings. Many other examples of relationship make the same point: the relationship between a parent and a child; the relationship between two children long before sexual differentiation is an issue; the relationship between persons pursuing a common goal (such as discovering a cure for AIDS or winning the National League pennant race); the relationship of love between Fred and Mary; the relationship of love between Fred and Joe; or the relationship of love between Mary and Sue.

While the relationship of "male and female" can be richly satisfying and enduring, it is only one example. Indeed, there are occasions when the relationship of male and female can produce hell on earth—two people in the process of destroying each other—and occasions when the relationship between two women or between two men can be richly satisfying and enduring in ways some heterosexual relationships never approach. It is unthinkable that God would create a world expressly designed for the experience of relationship, and then insist that only one kind of relationship—one that many people have no chance to experience—meets all the requirements.

So we must take the Genesis reference to "male and female" as illustrative of something that is not limited to married heterosexuals, but that can be experienced by many others as well, in a variety of rich relationships where the power of both human love and divine love are experienced. All of which suggests that our text is really saying, "God created human beings in God's own image; in the image of God, God created them, *for relationship* God created them." Rather than excluding most people, such a reading opens the door to include "all sorts and conditions" of men and women, and affirms that in the highest expression of human relationship—whatever form that takes—we get our clearest understanding of God and of each other. Here is where divine love and human love cannot finally be separated. The Taizé liturgy has a refrain that goes:

> Ubi caritas et amor,
> ubi caritas,
> Deus ibi est,

which we may translate, "Where love is present, there too God is present." That is the heart of the matter.

III

Third surprise: our churches are having trouble with all this. Actually, that's hardly cause for surprise anymore. Every branch of the Christian family—Catholic, Protestant, Orthodox—is besieged with problems having to do not only with homosexuality but with sexuality itself. We can use the Presbyterian Church as a handy example of the strains and stresses that are visible everywhere.

On Election Day in 1992, the people of Oregon rejected a ballot measure that would have encouraged gay bashing and mandated negative treatment of homosexuality in the schools. The secular society refused to sanction further oppression of gays and lesbians. Ironically, the very next day, the Judicial Council of the Presbyterian Church (the highest church court, beyond which there is no institutional appeal save to God) voted 11 to 1 that the Rev. Jane Spahr, a woman ordained in 1976, could not accept a call to be a pastor in the Downtown Presbyterian Church of Rochester, New York. Was this because she had turned out to be a poor preacher, an inefficient administrator, a noncaring pastor? No. Her call was declared null and void solely because the Rev. Jane Spahr is lesbian, and had had the courage to say so publicly. No other reason was advanced. No other reason was needed. And so the church, in contrast to the secular society, voted overwhelmingly to approve further oppression of gays and lesbians within the church.

The constitutional standards of the Presbyterian Church have wonderful statements about diversity and inclusivity in membership. When new members join, the constitutional standards are clear: they become part of the membership *and ministry* of the church. Even more specifically, they are "entitled to all the rights and privileges of the church including the right . . . to vote and *hold office*" (italics added).

But the practice of the church falls far short of such generosity. Despite what the constitutional standard states, all persons are entitled to hold office *except homosexuals,* since a General Assembly in 1978 had stated that "unrepentant homosexual practice does not accord with the requirements for ordination."

What channels, if any, are still open to the many gays and lesbians who feel called by God to an ordained ministry in the church of Jesus Christ? In effect, they are presented with three options, not one of them creative, all of them cruel:

1. They can *repent* of the "sin" of homosexuality, which they claim is not a sin, since God made them that way. No help there.
2. They can acknowledge their sexual orientation but promise to *remain celibate*—a requirement for ordination that characterizes Roman Catholic polity, but has never been part of the Protestant understanding of ministry. No help there, either.
3. They can *lie.* They can hide who they really are, pretend to be straight even though they are gay, and live an untruth throughout their ministry, a ministry to honor one who said, "I am the . . . truth." The most morally distasteful of all.

It takes little reflection to see how repugnant such demands are to gays and lesbians themselves, and how lacking in integrity they ought to appear to others.

What our churches say to gays and lesbians is that the real message of Genesis and of the gospel is that some, but not all, people are made in God's image; gays and lesbians are excluded. They are second-class citizens at best, and by denying them the right to ordination, the churches are telling them that they are second-class Christians as well.

Both as a human being, and as one whose ministry has been validated by ordination, I find these conclusions demeaning and cruel and unchristian.

IV

None of that is going to change in any denomination in the near future. (The best the Presbyterians could do at the 1993 General Assembly was a decision to "study the matter" for three years, under conditions making gay and lesbian participation virtually impossible.) Christians who want change are not advised to hold their breath while waiting its arrival. So what lies ahead?

Those who disapprove of their denomination's present stand must find one another and organize, keeping up the pressure for change no matter how numerically unlikely such change seems at present. ("Here we stand," might be their cry, "we can do no other. God help us!") The churches' tediously slow disavowal of slavery as God's will is ironically encouraging in the long view, if not the short.

Some congregations and lower judicatories may decide to engage in ecclesiastical disobedience, refusing to be bound by "official" decisions they feel are patently contrary to God's will. This might involve ordaining homosexuals or blessing same-sex unions in the church.

Those who engage in such intramural protest must accept the likelihood that official charges will be brought against them. In any risk taking, we have it on high authority that it is important to "count the cost" ahead of time, and work out strategies that will win support rather than harden opposition. But a time may come when the only creative option left is to leave.

This does not mean becoming single-issue churches. Full rights for homosexuals is surely a justice issue but it is not the only justice issue. Churches committed to rights for homosexuals must continue to work for the rights of the homeless, the exploited, the oppressed, in the same way they have done before. Social justice issues are interrelated, and to embrace one is finally to embrace them all, allowing for different emphases from time to time. This means hanging in for the long haul.

Why? Because, to come full circle, we believe along with Genesis that everyone *without exception* is made in God's image. If human and divine relationships are the crux of the matter, then we need to nurture and sustain one another, knowing that all of us are being nurtured and sustained by God as well.

And let the people say, "Amen!"

Scandal, Justice, Pearl Harbor, and Other Related Items, Including "a Refiner's Fire"

Reading: Malachi 2:17–3:4

Text: But who may abide the day of his coming? and who shall stand when he appeareth? for he is like a refiner's fire.—Malachi 3:2

The book of Malachi is not one to which we turn frequently. Malachi's situation is the following: The Jews have come back from the exile and resettled in Palestine, but things are not going well. In particular, maintaining the temple cult is expensive, and the Every Member Canvass is bogged down; only 62 percent of last year's pledges have been renewed. To make things worse, the sorcerers are raking in a big haul in the marketplaces, the rich are oppressing the poor once again, and widows and orphans are getting the short end of the stick as usual. Snafu—situation normal, all fouled up. Malachi tries to speak to these assorted ills:

> You have wearied God with your talk. You ask, "How have we wearied him?" By saying that all evildoers are good in the eyes of God, that God is pleased with them, or by asking, "Where is the God of justice?" I am about to send my messenger to clear a path before me. Suddenly the God whom you seek will come to the temple; the messenger of the covenant in whom you delight is here, here already, says the God of Hosts. Who can endure the day of his coming? Who can stand firm when he appears? He is like a refiner's fire, like a fuller's soap; he will take his seat, testing and purifying; he will purify the Levites and refine them like gold and silver, and so they will be fit to bring offerings to God. Thus the offerings of Judah and Jerusalem will be pleasing to God as they were in former days, in years long past. (Malachi 2:17–3:4)

If the words of the text ring a bell, it is probably because we are familiar with Handel's *Messiah,* and are aware that the words come early on as a bass solo, followed by a recitative, also by the bass, in which the heavens, the earth, the sea, the dry lands, and all the nations are "shaken," as only a bass recitative can shake them. The following solo, "But who may abide the day of his coming and who shall stand when he appeareth?" is gentle and yearning. But the solo is overtaken by a wild passage, "For he is like a refiner's fire, and who shall stand when he appeareth?" The question answers itself: not many. The plaintive melody returns but once again the refiner's fire simply won't go away. The following chorus, "And he shall purify," makes clear that being purified isn't going to be much fun.

In the midst of all this, the people are complaining that the bad guys are getting away with it, that they can do evil and God does nothing. So their question is, "Where is the God of justice?" which is another way of asking, "Who's minding the store?" But when God replies that somebody is already on the way, it's not, so to speak, reassuring.

I

The first theme that emerges out of this volatile situation is one of *scandal*. The transcendent God, high and lifted up, is about to put in an appearance. "You're asking where the God of justice is? Allow me to introduce myself."

There is no way that that can be good news. No sane person is going to respond, "Splendid. Allow me to introduce myself, too." The response is going to be something like, "Maybe we could negotiate some other terms for your arrival? Look, we can explain why giving in the temple is not up to snuff. You know as well as we do, O God, that we're in the midst of a recession that hasn't bottomed out yet, and money is tight all around. . . . What's that? You're not as interested in the temple offerings as you are in some other things? . . . No, don't start itemizing our shortcomings, or if you must, at least itemize somebody else's first." And God replies, "My messenger is on the way."

Then the messenger asks a couple of rhetorical questions about the promised appearance of God, "Who can endure the day of his coming? Who can stand firm when he appears?" The anticipated answer is "Nobody." And nobody challenges the anticipated answer. Nobody wants to be the one who stands—ever so lonely—against a God who seems to have an agenda full of demands. For the coming of God, the messenger forewarns, will be like the coming of a refiner's fire—an experience most of us would rather postpone until a more propitious time.

We want God to put in an appearance? Certainly! But on *our* terms, please, not God's. We want comfort and solace in the midst of tough times, which these days certainly are, and God is talking about justice. . . . By this time, somebody in the crowd must have queried, "Who asked that crazy question about 'Where is the God of justice?'" Wherever such a God is, let us hope God is content to stay there.

If God is scandalized by our behavior, we are scandalized by God's behavior. How dare God call us to account for what we have done with our lives? How dare God imply that we've got to change and change drastically, so that talk of a "refiner's fire" sounds both scary and likely. G. K. Chesterton, a British man of letters, caught the universal dilemma nicely, "Children are innocent and love justice; while most of us are wicked and naturally prefer mercy."

So the question of the people, "Where is the God of justice?" is not a question we want to ask lightly. The answer might be, "I'm on my way." A scandalous notion.

II

This leads us from the Temple Square in Jerusalem in 460 B.C. right up to the present day. Members of my generation can answer the question, "Where were you when you heard about Pearl Harbor?" The next generation can answer the question, "Where were you when you heard that President Kennedy had been shot?" And the youngsters (at least those in California) can answer the question, "Where were you on October 7, 1989, at 5:07 P.M. when the earthquake struck?" Those are all moments that cast light on what came before and what will come after. So let us reflect on the fiftieth anniversary of Pearl Harbor in the light of the question in Malachi, "Where is the God of justice?"

Pearl Harbor was a terrible event. A lot of people died, most of them horribly, most of them Americans in the bombed battleships, but some of them Japanese in the planes that bombed the battleships. But Pearl Harbor was terrible in other ways as well—most of all in the legacy it left—the way in which U.S. anger against the pilots of the planes was skillfully fanned into hatred against an entire people. I remember a song, only days after Pearl Harbor, that was soon on every radio: "We're gonna have to slap/the dirty yellow Jap/and Uncle Sam's the guy/who can do it." Response: cheers for us, jeers for them, and long lines at the recruitment stations. There may have been legitimate aims in World War II, but they didn't initially include hatred, and after Pearl Harbor they did.

Much of this is understandable in wartime. Your two sons are killed at Pearl Harbor and you don't have very generous thoughts about the killers. But there are two further consequences of Pearl Harbor that we need to remember.

The *first* is that many Americans have tried to keep the hatred alive ever since, and the fiftieth anniversary of Pearl Harbor has given those folks new life. They claim that the people who failed to defeat us militarily in the 1940s are defeating us economically in the 1990s, and it's all their fault. This is called Japan bashing. The economy is in trouble? Blame the Japanese. U.S. car sales are down? Blame the Japanese. We are losing our competitive edge in the electronics industry? Blame the Japanese. That is an ugly part of the legacy of Pearl Harbor, and the worse the economy gets the worse Japan bashing is likely to become. It is compounded by making the word "Jap" an epithet like nigger, or kike, or gook. There is no place for that in the vocabulary of any Christian.

In addition to Japan bashing, there is a *second* legacy of Pearl Harbor. It is not only what happened then, but what we as a nation have done since then. One of these actions was very close to us here in California—the setting up of so-called relocation centers complete with barbed wire and command posts with machine guns (just like the German concentration camps) that were used to house 120,000 American citizens—repeat, American citizens—who happened to be of Japanese ancestry. Years of people's lives, whole lifetimes of savings, homes, farms, self-respect, were recklessly wrenched from them.

We, not the Japanese, created the atomic bomb, and in dropping one such bomb on Hiroshima we killed 70,000 people, at least thirty times the number of all those killed at Pearl Harbor, and two days later we dropped a second atomic bomb on Nagasaki.

I need to say a little more about Nagasaki, because Lt. (jg) R. M. Brown, ChC, USNR #446549, was in Nagasaki only a few months after the destruction. We went by train from our ship, anchored in Sasebo Harbor, and I was surprised when the train stopped out in the barren countryside, and we were told it was the end of the line. Then I realized that this had been downtown Nagasaki before the bomb. Nagasaki was in a bowl or basin surrounded by hills, so that there had not only been the original explosion, but the massive sound waves that bounced back from the surrounding hills and hit the city a second time, leveling still more buildings in their wake. There was *nothing there* until we got into the area of the city that had been hit only by conventional bombs. There were damaged buildings, twisted frames, massive amounts of rubble still not cleared away, and who knows how many thousands of dead still not unearthed. I was in uniform, and I felt sadness and embarrassment and shame.

I know the conventional wisdom: the atomic bombs ended the war. But after one look at Nagasaki, I began to reflect that we could have made the point about the bomb's destructive capacity by announcing that we would drop one on an uninhabited area, and let Japanese inspection teams relay its mute message of destruction. And even if there could have been justification for dropping the first bomb on Hiroshima, there was no excuse whatever—moral, military, or psychological—for dropping the second one on densely populated Nagasaki, the one whose destructiveness I saw at first hand. Japan was already suing for peace.

The story goes on. In 1946 we dropped an atomic bomb on a flotilla of ships gathered around the Bikini atoll, to see what the bomb could do in such a situation. It did plenty. Before the test we forcibly removed the islanders who lived on Bikini, and they have never been able to go back, because of the radioactive fallout. (My ship was the last to leave Bikini before the explosion, and everybody wanted to go with us, since nobody knew what would happen when the bomb was exploded.) What subsequently happened, over forty years, was that as we and the other nuclear powers conducted tests near to Pacific islands, we built up so much radioactivity that today when women in that part of the Pacific have babies, a large percentage of them are what are called "jellyfish" babies, grotesque distortions of human beings who, mercifully, live only a few hours.

That's our track record.

When it became known recently that Japan was considering making a formal apology for Pearl Harbor, our President was asked if he would reciprocate with a formal apology for Hiroshima and Nagasaki. The reply was a flat No—there would be no statement of remorse, no apology, no confession of wrongdoing from the United States. Since we would not make a statement, the Japanese decided not to make a statement either. A great historical opportunity was lost. How wonderful it would have been in the history of international relations if both the United States and Japan could mutually have acknowledged that there were terrible sins on *both* sides, and that we both were promising to see that they never happened again. (At the very least, the United States had previously indicated wrongdoing in the internment of Americans of Japanese descent and paid out token sums in retribution.)

What this long recital means, in terms of the question in Malachi, "Where is the God of justice?" is that it is not enough to say *only* that God condemns the injustice of what happened at Pearl Harbor—as I am sure God does. The questions must also be answered in terms of divine condemnation for the injustice of the concentration camps, of Hiroshima, of Nagasaki, of Bikini, and of "jellyfish" babies. It is not anti-American to say that. It is simply one of the consequences of being (as we claim to be) "one nation under God." Such a nation stands under the judgment as well as the mercy of God.

III

This brings us back to Malachi's "refiner's fire," in which the goldsmith or silversmith heats the metal to get rid of impurities, to make the created objects more beautiful. That is an image that can help us relate the imperious demands of the God of justice to the unexpected gifts of the God of mercy—one God, not two.

A refiner's fire hurts as it burns away the dross, the imperfections. But its purpose is not to hurt, its purpose is to purify, to cleanse, to heal. So the refiner's fire is finally a symbol of *hope,* that what is presently hidden can be revealed, that what is potential can become actual, that what is now ugly can become beautiful.

That's not too bad a description of who we are—good things (very good, very precious things) who have somehow gotten spoiled—misdirected by hatred or shortsightedness, or failure to see the good in others. And every now and then, something happens on the human scene that provides suggestive evidence that there *is* a goodness that the refiner's fire can reveal. I offer two examples.

Many of us saw on television the scene of a seventy-two-year-old retired U.S. seaman who survived Pearl Harbor, and recently visited the Pearl Harbor memorial at the sunken U.S.S. *Arizona.* A Japanese man came up to him, took his hand and said, "I'm sorry," and then embraced him, saying through tears, "I'm so sorry for what we did." And the American seaman returned the embrace of the Japanese man, and through his own tears said, "Thank you." Fifty years of hatred neutralized and destroyed, because they had both been through the refiner's fire and were new beings.

Even more graphic, perhaps, were the words of ex-hostage Terry Anderson, only three days out of a refiner's fire of over six years in captivity. Asked whether he hated his captors, Terry Anderson said clearly and directly, "I don't hate anybody. I'm a Christian and a Catholic and I really believe that. And it's required of me that I forgive, no matter how hard that may be. And I'm determined to do that."

Our faith challenges us to look at ourselves as those in need of refinement, of coming to terms with our own excesses or distortions, that keep us from being who we truly want to be. So let us accept the scandal of the initial frightening possibility of God coming into our world—and use it to discover things about ourselves that really need that refining fire, welcoming the intrusion of God's justice as a necessary preparation for the gift of God's mercy.

O God, you approach us in many ways—sometimes as judge, sometimes as redeemer, sometimes as justice, sometimes as mercy. Help us to accept what seems the sterner side of your coming, in faith that you are *for* us rather than against us, the one who, if we will let you, will empower us to become more like what you originally intended us to be. In Jesus' name. Amen.

– 20 –

Sacrifice—
and the Federal Budget

Reading: Matthew 4:1–11

A big event has been taking place in the desert. While John the Baptist—a kind of first-century Billy Graham—is giving an altar call "down by the riverside" on the banks of the Jordan, a young man named Jesus presents himself for baptism. John sizes him up and suggests that Jesus should be baptizing him rather than the other way around. (At this point the Billy Graham analogy begins to limp.) But Jesus prevails on John to lay aside his scruples, and the baptism takes place, with such added attractions as a descending dove (symbolizing the Holy Spirit, so Matthew informs us in the spirit of helpfulness), and a voice from heaven saying, clear as a bell, "This is my beloved Son [capital S] in whom I take delight."

Following this spiritual and emotional high, Jesus disappears into a nearby desert to figure out what it all means. He has clearly been assigned an important role in the life of his people, for "Son of God [with a capital S]" is a messianic title, not to be claimed or accepted lightly.

The account of Jesus' search for clarification in the desert must go back to Jesus himself, since no one else was there to observe or take notes except for an antagonist, variously called a "devil" and a "tempter." The ensuing encounter is an intense inner struggle within Jesus to discover what kind of a Messiah he is supposed to be. He externalizes the inner pulls and pushes in what is a vivid symbolic drama in three acts. The curtain rises:

Jesus was then led by the Spirit into the wilderness, to be tempted by the devil.

For forty days and nights he fasted, and at the end of them he was famished. The tempter approached him and said, "If you are the Son of God, tell these stones to become bread." Jesus answered, "Scripture says, 'We are not to live on bread alone, but on every word that comes from the mouth of God.' "

The devil then took him to the Holy City and set him on the parapet of the temple. "If you are the Son of God," he said, "throw yourself down; for

Scripture says, "God will put the angels in charge of you, and they will support you in their arms, for fear you should strike your foot against a stone.' "
Jesus answered him, "Scripture also says, 'You are not to put your God to the test.' "

The devil took him next to a very high mountain, and showed him all the kingdoms of the world in their glory. "All these," he said, "I will give you, if you will only fall down and do me homage." But Jesus said, "Out of my sight, Satan! Scripture says, 'You shall do homage to God and worship God alone.' "

Then the devil left him; and angels came and attended to his needs. (Matthew 4:1–11)

Let us begin far from the river Jordan, with the most immediately present reality in our lives as U.S. citizens—the presentation of a presidential budget, and ask what it has to do with the living of the Christian life.

A few disclaimers are in order. I will not offer an economic appraisal of the budget, such as proposing a different ratio between cuts and expenditures. I will not suggest that there is an *explicit* Christian wisdom about details of the budget. Nor will I imply that all Christians (or even all Presbyterians) ought to agree with where I come out. Nor, finally, am I going to assign particular blame for the fix we are in. If I refer to "the baleful legacy of the last twelve years," that is not intended to be simply an unkind swipe at two of our most recent presidential incumbents, for during those twelve years we not only had a Republican White House but a Democratic Congress as well. There is enough blame to go around without having to apportion it between elephants and donkeys.

I

Our starting point *as Christians* in dealing with the budget is quite clear: we are called upon to make "*a preferential option for the poor.*" The phrase— now a familiar one in Catholic social teaching—is a kind of summary of God's activity in the biblical story, in which God is always found on the side of the poor and dispossessed. This does not mean that God hates the rich, or that there is an *exclusive* "option for the poor" to the neglect of everyone else, but that God's first, though not last, concern is for those who are on the bottom of the heap. And if that is where God is, that is where God's people, both individually and collectively, are supposed to be also, in solidarity with the victims.

This means that in approaching any federal budget, this year or next year, we as Christians cannot ask initially, "What's in it for us?" or, "Can't we find a loophole that will make our own participation less onerous?" Somewhere along the way, since we live in a fallen world, we will almost certainly ask such questions, whether we should or not, but our initial questions must center on whether a given proposal helps or hinders the poor and impoverished. This is doubly important when, as is so often the case, the poor and impoverished turn out to be people of another race or class than our own, about whom the general public couldn't care less. And since folks like us have an inordinate percentage of goods and capital and economic opportunities, part of the task of any budget must be to express special concern for the victims and provide a helping hand. This will impact how we assess health care proposals, education allotments, the ratio of cuts in defense to rebuilding the inner cities, and whether an energy tax will help or hinder the financial stability of a family on the margin of bare survival.

It is never easy to take such priorities seriously, but we must keep trying to do so, not only because they are morally demanded of us but also because so few other groups in society see that as their task.

II

A second reflection is suggested by one patently clear phrase, *no quick fixes,* and one distressingly necessary word, "sacrifice."

It will be folly to assume that if a decent budget can somehow be gotten through Congress we will have solved the budget crisis. We will have made only a modest start on a process that will have to continue painfully for many years. This means not setting our hopes impossibly high, but also not becoming so cynical that we lose the impetus for reforms that are doable. It will be a long, hard process. There will be a lot of inefficiency and a lot of graft along the way. Certain proposals will work, others won't. Some proposals will demand more capital than had been anticipated. A few may bring us one inch closer to creating a more just society. Throughout, we must recognize that there will be no quick fixes.

This means accepting the fact that there is no such thing as a budgetary free lunch. A word has emerged on the scene that the realists claim sends bad vibes. It is the word "sacrifice," and let's not throw it out too quickly. Sacrifice is an important word in the Christian vocabulary, even though it is not a word around which we ever rally enthusiastically, for it has overtones of hardship, suffering, and being trampled on. Nobody campaigns for public office on a platform extolling sacrifice. But it is still part of our heritage, and we must examine it.

In the earliest times, people offered sacrifices—usually animals—to the gods as a means of getting on the right side of the particular divinity's favor and securing its forgiveness. Such an understanding became increasingly manipulative as a way to "buy" God's approval by the splendor of one's offering. ("You sacrificed a bullock? *I* sacrificed three!") The whole system was roundly attacked by Amos and his prophetic friends, who helped transform the notion of sacrifice into the offering not of an animal but of *oneself* to God by the doing of justice. God says to Amos, to be relayed to the people, "I hate, I despise your offerings. They do not please me. Instead of them, let justice roll down like waters, and righteousness like a mighty stream" (Amos 5:24). The psalmist sings to God, "You take no delight in sacrifices; were I to bring a burnt offering, you would not accept it. The sacrifice acceptable to you is a broken and contrite heart" (Ps. 51:16–17), which clearly means a heart turned away from concern for self and devoted to concern for the other. The true worship, the true sacrifice, Isaiah says, is "to loose the bonds of wickedness, to undo the thongs of the yoke, to let the oppressed go free; to share bread with the hungry, to care for the homeless poor, and satisfy the needs of the afflicted" (Isaiah 58, passim), a massive agenda.

An amazing thing has happened. Sacrifice, which was initially a way of ingratiating oneself before God, has acquired a brand-new meaning: making oneself available to the victims, sharing one's goods with those who have no goods, working to restructure an unjust society. And that is costly. To be blunt about it, if we are committed to such concerns, then most of us will have to pay higher taxes. That will be a part, at least, of our sacrifice. We will not only have to bear our own burdens, we will have to bear a portion of our neighbors' burdens as well. This doesn't give us special wisdom about how the burdens should be shared—those details will be hammered out in congressional committees. But acceptance of the fact that many of us are going to have to pay more than in the past will either be acknowledged by us voluntarily or thrust upon our grandchildren coercively.

III

A third comment about faith and the budget sounds initially like far-fetched pious talk, but it is the most important point of all: *we must give our primary allegiance to God.* Easy to say from the pulpit, tough to do from the pew. But look at it this way: as a congregation, we have accumulated *some* wisdom about God, out of our weekly worship here, and for *today* the thing we most need to remember out of all our communal experience is that to love God—which is what worship is all about—means to love one another, and that means to *care* for one another. We do a lot of caring one-on-one, and we do it pretty well. In relation to the budget, however, worshiping the true God means also that we care for one another *through the structures in our society,* whether we are talking about health insurance, child care, Head Start programs, protection for the elderly, or tough legislation that makes bigotry too expensive to be practical. We have ways to accomplish at least some of those otherwise impossibly demanding tasks. We are mandated by our faith to put increasing pressure on our elected officials, making clear what we *want,* what we will work to *support,* what we will at least *tolerate,* and what we will vehemently *oppose.* In such ways we care for the neighbor; in such ways we glorify God.

Can we tie all that into what happened between two antagonists in a wilderness twenty centuries ago? (Let's not press for too tidy correlations; we are not, like Jesus, trying to figure out how to be a Messiah. If we are, we need more help than will be forthcoming in the next three minutes.) But there are some connections.

For Jesus, who was understandably famished after fasting forty days and nights, the first temptation was to use *his* God-given powers for himself, make bread out of stones and satisfy his own immediate need. For us, the task is simply to use *our* God-given powers to see that bread is not only baked, but that it gets to everyone who lacks it. That's a quick definition of a preferential option for the poor.

For Jesus, the temptation to jump off the temple and land unscathed was the temptation to be a wonder-working Messiah, to offer a wide-screen spectacular any time he took a drop in the polls, to validate his message by being a bungee jumper without a rope and still landing safely. For us, such a temptation is a reminder that we don't have the resources to pull off wide-screen spectaculars even if we want to. We must believe that despite no quick fixes, the ultimate resource of sacrifice (redefined) is our best resource in the desert or out of it.

For Jesus, the temptation to get control of the world by selling out to the forces of evil must have been particularly tempting: *Do evil that good may come.* This is the most insidious of all moral temptations. We all face it: cheat on our income tax, use phony arguments to win political debates, make promises we know we can't keep, spread rumors about the private lives of our opponents on public issues—all the while claiming that the ends justify such means.

In the face of that, let the message of the morning be that our inner concerns and our outer actions cannot be separated. If that seems less than self-evident, read further in the temptation account and see what Jesus did after his inner struggle and his return to the world of outer actions.

Once Jesus chose some helpers, Matthew reports, "he traveled throughout Galilee, teaching in the synagogues, proclaiming the good news of the kingdom, and healing every kind of illness and infirmity among the people. And they brought to him sufferers from various diseases . . . and he healed them all" (Matt. 4:23–24).

Concentrate on that latter activity for just a moment. If you have that kind of healing gift yourself, you'd better get busy. But if you don't, and think such healing is important, you can become a healer by joining with others to make sure that our nation develops a plan for medical assistance that reaches every single citizen. That way, you're not only engaging in political activity, you are also sharing in Jesus' ongoing ministry of healing at the same time.

God, it's a difficult time to be alive, but it is also an exciting time. We thank you for placing us in the here and now. Despite lots of discouragement, we also see encouraging signs along the way. We can dare to hope. There are tasks to do. There are means with which to do them. Empower us to get on with the job. For Jesus' sake. Amen.

Part 4
Coda: Death and Life

"Coda" is a familiar musical term to denote the concluding section of a musical composition, in which the composer brings various thematic concerns to a formal closure. This may be appropriate for a musician, but it is much too confining for a theologian, whose work must always communicate a sense of incompletion, pointing to something either left unsaid by the author or waiting to be said better by another author. I retain the word even so, both to signal a formal ending to the present conversation, and to signal as well that the ongoing overall conversation continues. The final word about the interaction of death and life will never be spoken or written by any mortal. Our words are tiny pointers. Nothing more.

– 21 –

Giving Thanks
in the Midst of Death?

Reading: Colossians 1:11–20
Text: In God's glorious might may God give you ample strength to meet with fortitude and patience whatever comes; and give joyful thanks to God.—Colossians 1:11–12

The lectionary reading is a paean of praise by Paul, about Christ's presence in the whole of creation and especially in the church. If the language sometimes sounds extravagant, that is only because Paul's faith is extravagant, overflowing with gratitude and exaltation. I stress the upbeat mood because the letter is written from prison, and there is nothing quite as effective in dampening an upbeat mood as being incarcerated. But Paul has looked adversity in the face and refuses to give it the last word:

> In God's glorious might may God give you ample strength to meet with fortitude and patience whatever comes; and give joyful thanks to God, who has made you fit to share the heritage of God's people in the realm of light.
>
> God rescued us from the domain of darkness and brought us into the realm of God's own Son, through whom our release is secured and our sins are forgiven. Christ is the image of the invisible God; his is the primacy over all creation. In him everything in heaven and on earth was created, not only things visible but also the invisible orders of thrones, sovereignties, authorities, and powers; the whole universe has been created through him and for him. He exists before all things, and all things are held together in him.
>
> He is the head of the body, the church. He is its origin, the first to return from the dead to become in all things supreme. For in him all God's fullness chose to dwell, and through him to reconcile all things to God. (Colossians 1:11–20)

So here is the substance of Paul's message: "May God give you ample strength to meet with fortitude and patience whatever comes; and give joyful thanks to God."

Let's put that advice squarely within two events of our own immediate situation. Last week we suffered a tragedy in Jim Burnett's unnecessary death in an auto accident. To deal with this we need all the "fortitude" and "patience" Paul can supply. And this week we are celebrating the annual festival of Thanksgiving, when we are supposed to be "joyful" and "thankful."

And those two things don't fit together. We're not joyful, we're angry. We're not thankful, we're resentful. How can we give thanks in the midst of death?

I

An initial response comes not from the Pauline text but from the text of human experience, which coincides with the Hebrew Scriptures. It goes like this: in such situations, *it's okay to be angry with God.* That's not part of the received Protestant heritage, in which anger is almost always a no-no. Christians don't get angry, Christians love and forgive. Christians seek reconciliation not conflict. And anyhow, who are we to question the ways of God? What arrogance!

But wait a minute. The theme of being upset, even outraged, at what God does is a venerable theme within scripture. The quintessential instance is Jeremiah, who spent his whole life contesting with God over how God was running the universe and what unfair things God was demanding of Jeremiah. Jeremiah was angry at what he saw and addressed his complaint to God, "Why does the way of the wicked prosper? Why do all who are treacherous survive?" (Jer. 12:1). Job has the same response: the roof of his entire universe caves in, flocks gone, houses gone, sons destroyed, a terrible case of boils, and nothing to do but sit on a dump heap and scratch and complain. Job is outraged. What did *he* do to deserve such calamities? What kind of God is it, anyway, who lets such injustice go unchecked?

Such responses at least take God seriously. The one who says in effect, "Yes, there's a lot of suffering in God's universe but we'll just have to accept it without complaint," is trivializing God, living on the assumption that God doesn't really matter.

Instead of that we are invited, along with Job and Jeremiah, to voice our complaints. And if we do, honestly and searchingly, an extraordinary thing happens. It is best said by Pedro, a character in Elie Wiesel's *The Town Beyond the Wall.* In the Spanish Civil War, Pedro has seen his partner raped thirty-seven times by the enemy and then discarded—nothing but a mutilated corpse. In the face of all that Pedro says to a friend (and I retain the sexist language so that the point is not lost), "I want to blaspheme [against

God] and I can't quite manage it. I go up against Him, I shake my fist, I froth with rage, but it's still a way of telling Him that He is there, that He exists, that my very denial is an offering to His grandeur. The shout becomes a prayer in spite of me" (p. 123).

Anger can be appropriate and even healing and cleansing, when it is moral outrage at the way things have gone. A death camp should make us outraged and asking, Where is God in a world where this can happen? An unnecessary death, like Jim Burnett's, should not leave us meekly acquiescing and showing our "faith" by not complaining. It *is* outrageous. It need not have happened. It should not have happened. It makes the whole human venture seem utterly capricious: Why Jim and not someone else? Why anyone at all, if the universe is as much under divine governance as Paul insists to the Colossians? There would be something wrong with us if we were not frequently morally outraged at what happens to people.

II

So it's okay to be angry with God. But we then have to ask, *Where do we go beyond anger?*

Well, for one thing we have to summon resources from wherever we find them, just to keep on going. Remember, once again, that Paul was writing from prison, and he gives counsel in *his* difficult situation to those in other kinds of difficult situations. We can ask God to give us, as he puts it, "ample strength to meet with fortitude and patience whatever comes." That may not be a recipe for getting answers to our questions, but it *is* a recipe for getting up in the morning, borrowing strength from friends, and continuing with the living of one's life.

Fortitude and patience, the two virtues Paul summons for us, are interesting and complementary. Fortitude is a strong word, kin to such words as fortify and strengthen, signaling the image of a fortress standing firm under attack. The dictionary gives some interesting synonyms: backbone, pluck, guts. And then, as though subliminally influenced by Paul, the dictionary goes on to say, "see also Patience," which is Paul's second word. *Patience* is a stronger word than we sometimes think. It's not just "enduring without complaint" (a trait often wrongly applied to Job, who was anything but "patient" in his situation). It means steadiness, endurance, calmness, control. A synonym out of our contemporary vocabularies might be "hanging in there."

There are ways beyond anger, and we need to explore them because we cannot keep anger finely honed indefinitely. If we rely ultimately on anger to keep us going, it festers and turns into hatred, which dehumanizes not only those to whom it is directed, but also those who inflict it.

When we try to move beyond anger in Christian terms, we find that we are asking questions that grow not only out of our experience but also out of the experiences of others, especially when we confront the ultimate challenge of death. We are part of a communal venture.

In the heritage of that communal venture we find two apparently conflicting attitudes toward death. On the one hand, death is seen as the final *enemy*, the implacable foe against which we exert all our energy, hoping somehow to lessen its power. We feel its utter negativity particularly in the case of the death of children, or any death, like Jim's, that comes too soon. We want our lives to be free of the visitation of death, especially to those we love. So death is the ultimate challenge to the meaningfulness of life, to the notion that beyond all mystery, love dwells as conqueror.

But there is also a strain in our faith that sees death as *part of life*, of the great cycle of ourselves, our environment, our universe—something that is inescapably ordained for everyone, which, if we are fortunate, we may find it possible to approach with calmness and without fear. This attitude "works," in those cases where someone lives out the fullness of his or her appointed years into old age and dies peacefully. But it is only a tiny fraction of the human family who are given such a possibility. Fifteen thousand times a day it doesn't work. That is the number of people who will starve to death on this planet in the next twenty-four hours. Nor does it work for the Jim Burnetts, whose deaths seem to be sheer caprice, as lacking in meaning as their lives were full of meaning.

Our clue here, as Christians, comes from Paul's descriptive reference to Jesus in the letter to the Colossians. Out of many titles for Jesus available to Paul by the A.D. 60s, when the letter was written, Paul chooses to describe Jesus simply as "the first to return from the dead." The assumption is that Jesus is not exempted from death any more than the rest of us. In fact, he dies a more grisly and painful death than most human beings do. If we look into the face of Jesus, we see (whatever else we see) a doomed convict, found guilty in the courts of law of his day, and killed with efficient Roman dispatch. Death is no stranger to him.

Now what happens next in the Jesus story is clearly the most important part, and the part that is most difficult for us to believe as modern women and men. Set aside the *details* of the resurrection accounts, which conflict at many points, and the picture is less confused. But set aside the claim to which the details point, and we have set aside the Christian faith. For, by whatever vocabulary and imagery we choose, it is absolutely *central* to the Christian story that death was not the end for Jesus. We can let go parts of the Jesus story (some of the miracles, perhaps, and a good deal of hyperbole about walking on water or ushered into life accompanied by stars in the East) but central to the ongoing meaning of the Jesus story has been the claim that death is not the final victor over life. Grant me the word "Lord" just twice in this sermon: God is Lord of *life*, yes; but God is also Lord of *death*, meaning that God's love triumphs over evil's hatred.

That claim flies in the face of common sense and all sorts of evidence to the contrary. But a prime reason for the existence of this church, and those of us within it, is to keep alive the testimony that, as Paul says elsewhere, "Death is swallowed up in victory." If you let that go, you can lead a committed Stoic existence, saying in effect, "My defeat is sure but I will struggle against it as long as I can draw a breath," which is an honorable alternative to Christian faith. But that is not the Christian message, which goes, by contrast, "When I draw my last breath, I will find myself not forsaken and alone, but sustained and empowered and renewed in ways I cannot imagine. For I believe there is a power greater than death—the power of love, enduring all hardship and still conquering, the power of love shown in the face of Jesus Christ."

Yes, there are places to go beyond anger, and they involve fortitude and patience, and a fresh look at how our faith confronts its most challenging adversary.

III

Very well, we may say in moments of clarity, we'll go along with Paul on the need for fortitude and patience. But that next line in the text about thanksgiving? How can we be expected to live thankful lives in a universe that so brutally tramples down our hopes and dreams? In such situations isn't a national day of Thanksgiving mere whistling in the dark, trying to make us forget that the dark is real? How can Paul say so blithely, "Whatever comes . . . give joyful thanks to God"?

Let's do an inventory. Are there *some* things, even in the light of all the challenges we have to confront, for which we can give thanks?

For most of us there remains much for which to be thankful, although each of us will have a different list. But, we can all give thanks, for example, for the *life* of Jim Burnett, even as we deplore the fact and manner of his death. *He made a difference,* and we are grateful for him. Nothing can erase that fact. (When I got up here to preach two weeks ago about politics and the election, it suddenly seemed to me pretty thin gruel in the face of the fact that Jim was in the hospital in a coma, and his family was here in church, and I should surely have been preaching about our shared tragedy. But then I saw, very clearly in my mind's eye, Jim, telling me to go right ahead, encouraging me to preach about politics and the election, and even offering advice in his particular idiom about not being too tepid: *"Stick it to them, Robert!"*)

We can furthermore be grateful that none of us has to face the reality of the death of someone we love, alone. I do not think there could be much that would be worse than having to cope with the loss of someone we love, all by ourselves. There have been many deaths among those who worship in this church, and there will be more. And in every case, it is cause for gratitude that we are all part of a supportive community, and that we can count on that support from one another. Those who rally around us may sometimes seem awkward, or at a loss for words, or even too timid to approach us directly. But we know, from many years of being here, and from the strength of the embraces, that the prayers and the love and the concern of the whole family of the church are centered in on us when we need them. Let us never take such a reality for granted. Let us treasure it and hold fast to it. And what a community it is—a community in which, thanks to the presence of Jim Burnett, David Leith can (in a prayer at Jim's memorial service) identify "irreverence" as a virtue.

All of this is what, in the creeds and our hymns, is called the communion of saints—a community we feel right here, in *this* time and space, but also a community that transcends the boundaries of all time and space, including those who came before, and those we have loved who have stepped across that mysterious boundary, where their spirit and influence still live, even though their earthly bodies are hidden from us.

IV

In Psalm 139, the psalmist asks God, "Where can I escape from your spirit, where can I flee from your presence?" The psalm responds to the question in two syntactically parallel assertions. The first goes, in English, "If I climb up to heaven, behold you are there"—a rather obvious reply, for where else would God be? And the second one goes, in English, "If I make my bed in Sheol [the abode of the dead], behold you are there"—a reply that is not obvious at all, for the psalmist knows very well that Sheol is, by definition, the place where God is *not*. And as the writer starts to write in the Hebrew tongue about the presence of God even in Sheol, the vision is so overpowering that in some manuscripts the sentence stops in midstream, "If I make my bed in Sheol, behold thou . . . !" God in Sheol, totally unexpected, is the *reality*, beyond all definition, all logic, all syntax, all expectation—acquainting us with the glorious surprise that there is no place foreign to God's healing love and presence.

O God, sometimes you seem to demand more than we can bear and we get angry, or confused, or scared. Meet us more than halfway, we ask, and help us to cope with things that, without your power and presence, we could never handle. We know you desire good for us, so show us ways in which we can weave your love and compassion into the times in life that are difficult and often apparently impossible. Grant us help; through your Son who has walked the same pathway we walk, in whose name we pray. Amen.

– 22 –

Dear Mackenzie:
A Letter from the Depths

Readings: Ezekiel 37:1–14; Psalm 130
Text: In God love is unfailing,
and great is God's power to deliver.—Psalm 130:7

This sermon is about life and death. Not too surprisingly, so is the lectionary reading from Ezekiel. It is a famous, if somewhat fanciful, word picture about the Valley of Dry Bones. Hear it as a figure of speech—a simile or metaphor—about the great hope of life rising out of death, and don't worry overmuch about the prescientific mind-set.

Ezekiel, one of the great prophets of the Hebrew Scriptures, speaks:

God's hand was upon me, and God's spirit carried me out and set me down in a valley that was full of bones. Countless in number and very dry, they covered the valley. God said to me, "O man, can these bones live?" I answered, "Only you know that." God said, "Prophesy over these bones; say: Dry bones, hear the word of God. I am going to put breath into you and you will live. I shall fasten sinews on you, clothe you with flesh, cover you with skin, and give you breath and you will live. Then you will know that I am God."

I began to prophesy as I had been told, and as I prophesied there was a rattling sound and the bones all fitted themselves together. As I watched, sinews appeared upon them, flesh clothed them, and they were covered with skin, but there was no breath in them. Then God said to me, "Prophesy to the wind, O man, and say to it: These are the words of God: Let winds come from every quarter and breathe into these slain that they may come to life." I prophesied as I had been told; breath entered them, and they came to life, and rose to their feet, a mighty company. (Ezekiel 37:1–10)

Dear Mackenzie:

It begins to look as though you'll make it. I wouldn't have dared think so, let alone said so, a week ago. But I do now, cautiously and not too securely, realizing that a single setback could cancel out a dozen incremental gains. But I want to believe that God doesn't play cat-and-mouse games with us, at least not interminably. All those who love you have been on a psychic roller coaster, ever since your birth, fluctuating between initial joy and subsequent fear all tangled up together and difficult to unravel.

I want to try a bit of unraveling even so—when the outcome is not a sure thing—and tell you about a few of the things you have already done for those of us who love you, and will continue to love you, whether your life span is to be a few weeks or many years.

I

First of all, *you have widened the circle of love.* All sorts of people who never laid eyes on each other before are working together to save your life. They may not all employ the word "love" for what they do, but they embody love, and that's much more important. Some of them you'll never see again, and others will be focused on your life, and you on theirs, as long as anybody draws a breath. If you are ever tempted, later on, to think of your family as only a few relatives, we will remind you of your extended family, in there fighting for you even when a lot of them had not directly known you.

Who could have foreseen that when your father's students learned that you were in intensive care and needed more blood, thirty of them would independently go to the Oakland Blood Bank and offer theirs? In a new twist on an old phrase, you are being "saved by their precious blood." Who would have thought that a fourteen-year-old black student in your mother's class at Berkeley High, hearing that you were having kidney trouble would go to the teacher in the next room and ask, "How could I give one of my kidneys for Ms. Felix's sick baby?" Who could have anticipated the reality of the loving care by the entire hospital staff in the Pediatrics Intensive Care Unit, Floor Ten, Kaiser Hospital in Oakland? Or the phone calls, the cards, the promise of prayers, the reality of prayers? About all we could have anticipated for *sure* was that your mother and father would pass an unexpected crash course in parenthood with such flying colors.

All that, and more, Mackenzie, has happened because of you—not because you did something for all those people and they wanted to repay you, but simply because you *are* and you are in *need,* and you matter, and the love you represent calls out to be returned. And since we'd just as soon have learned about the love without the pain, maybe this will remind us next time to begin to exercise love toward one another without having to wait for a crisis to sensitize us.

The widening circle of human love reaches out beyond us, and includes a new awareness of the presence of the love of God. Never doubt, Mackenzie, that God's healing work is done through human hands, and that the laying on of hands is sacramental, whoever does it. When the large male nurse named Rich with infinite tenderness, lifts you from the bed where you are still attached to what seem like a dozen machines and monitors, and places you in your mother's or father's arms, saying that their embraces are as important as all the machines and monitors in restoring you to health—never doubt that God is present.

To most of us, God's presence is usually unspectacular—only a few are granted visions. It is so unspectacular, in fact, that we miss it most of the time. The breath of God has been breathed over you and into you (this is what we call God's Spirit) by every loving touch and gesture, whether those administering them are conscious of God in what they do or not. God takes whatever lies at hand and fashions it into something fresh and new.

Part of what has been keeping you alive is that incredible number of tubes and monitors and charts and respirators and dialysis machines all hooked up to you. I spend a fair amount of my professional time making caustic remarks about how technology wrongly shapes our lives. But when I first saw that mass of tubing encasing your tiny body I was not aggrieved but grateful, since I knew that every one of them was playing an assigned role in keeping you alive. Their function is to render themselves unnecessary, helping your tiny body begin to do what they are doing, so that you can gradually take over and permit their removal. And then, when you are unencumbered, you will be able, on your own, to breathe, to see, to laugh, to cry, to nurse, to smile.

You have widened the circle of love.

II

You have deepened the mysteries of love. There are things we will never understand, but within which we live. Here is one:

The mystery that what has happened to you is bad and yet good has come out of it. We can't make the bad good, but we can do things with it, like Tom's and Deb's students did. Instead of making us bitter, love can make us tender, and help us to focus outward on others going through comparable experiences: those other babies in intensive care, their parents, their doctors and nurses, and (perhaps especially) those millions of babies for whom no hospital care or life-prolonging devices are available. Out of the bad, much good can come, only we have to choose to make it that way. That is one of the mysteries of love.

Another mystery is this: what has been happening to you does funny things with how we think of time. In those first days in the hospital, when your parents were sleeping on the floor to be on hand and nobody knew whether you would make it through the next twenty-four hours, we discovered that *every day is a gift.* The words "Mackenzie is still alive" were sufficient for dancing in the streets. An announcement that there had been a slight—ever so slight—gain in your struggle was material for the music of angel choirs.

At some point, of course, we have to think not only about today but to plan for next week and next months. But in the Pediatrics Intensive Care Unit, we have learned to savor the moment.

W. H. Auden, a favorite poet of your grandfather, once gave the commencement address at Harvard University. He concluded a long speech in poetry with the words:

> If thou must choose
> Between the chances, choose the odd;
> Read *The New Yorker,* trust in God;
> And take short views.

I'll put my enthusiasm for *The New Yorker* on hold for the moment, and even defer for a few moments the advice to "trust in God." Instead, I'll just affirm the rightness of Auden's advice to "take short views."

Take short views. This means remembering that every day *is* a gift to be accepted for what it is, a set of boundless new possibilities. I hope that never again in our oh-so-busy lives will we forget what we learned in the Pediatrics Ward—the sheer wonder of a single day in which you, Mackenzie, and those we love, and all others elsewhere, are doing nothing more spectacular than breathing regularly. We should never fail to hold that up and cherish it as a gift of unparalleled worth.

You have widened the circle of love. You have deepened the mysteries of love.

III

You have exposed the vulnerability of love. This is the hardest one of all, Mackenzie, for to juxtapose love as assurance, and vulnerability as a threat to that assurance, is to acknowledge the fragility of everything we hold dear. You didn't *do* anything to create this situation, but simply by *being,* with the unavoidable possibility of not-being, you force us to examine things we would prefer not to confront.

To be vulnerable is to be woundable, to be susceptible to harm, and there is no way to avoid recognizing that for us to love you is to open ourselves to the possibility of loss; a time might come when you would no longer be around for us to love.

The greater the love, the greater the threat.

That's a possible conclusion and it seems unfair. Why should the greatest thing of all—love—be such an easy target for destruction? Some people shield themselves from that hard truth by avoiding deeply held commitments on the grounds that the potential price of such commitments is too costly, creating wounds that would be too deep.

But love means taking on those risks and saying with our lives, the risks are worth it because the rewards are so great, and better to possess love briefly than never to possess it at all.

The greater the love, the greater the fulfillment.

That's another possible conclusion and it seems worthwhile.

You have widened the circle of love. You have deepened the mysteries of love. You have exposed the vulnerability of love.

IV

And finally, *you have affirmed the reality of love.*

Would I be able to write these words if things were going badly? I'm not sure. I hope I could, but it would be a severe test. "Why," I would be asking myself if I were honest, "does all this happen to a tiny, newborn baby?"

I at least know, Mackenzie, that there is one answer that does not tempt me. It is to say (usually in pious tones), "Whatever happens is God's will and we must accept it."

No! I deny that. It is *not* God's will that you, or any of God's children, should suffer or die in infancy. It *is* God's will that you live joyously and fully. And that's what all the doctors and nurses and orderlies and machines and monitors are trying to bring about, whether the word "God" enters in or not. If you live, Mackenzie, we'll all give thanks to God in whatever ways we think of God. And if you don't live, we will refuse to be acquiescent and blindly accepting, and we'll have to believe somehow that God is present in the defeats as well as in the victories—a God who has chosen to be as vulnerable as we are, who feels pain as we do, who would mourn your loss as we would. Love and mystery and God remain intertwined.

I know at least that to affirm the reality of love is to look its opposite in the face, and do our best, throughout a lifetime, to stare it down. That activity, Mackenzie, is called *hope,* and we usually invoke it when things are rough and our spirits are sagging rather than soaring. It's a funny thing, hope is. Sometimes it's almost too scary to hope, for fear we will somehow put a hex on things, or that there will be a letdown worse than if we have never hoped at all, or even the crazy notion that we have to bargain with God, or fate, or whatever, in order to get grounds for hoping: "If you'll spare Mackenzie's life, I'll do x. And if you will also restore her to full health, I'll do x *and* y." I do not believe God wants us to operate that way, as though life and death were bargaining chips on a cosmic game board and all the dice were loaded.

I get my own hope, Mackenzie, from others—people stronger than I am, who have gone through the worst and, quite amazingly, still affirm. A long time ago some of those people compiled a songbook, and it's a great place to look when you are feeling weak. It has the formidable name of the Psalter, but that just means a "songbook," and the songwriters in it are important to me because they are so honest. Sometimes they are very joyful, and sometimes they are very sad. The best of them are both, and that's what counts.

In one of these songs, the writer says, "God, out of the *depths* have I cried to you," meaning a time when things were blackest and bleakest. The songwriter doesn't waste time griping, "Why did you let me get into this mess?" but instead utters a cry for help, "Wait for God with longing, I put my hope in God's [promises]." These words, or words like them, have been encircling your bed these past two weeks, Mackenzie. But that's not all, for the same writer who has been in the "depths" and waits in "longing," goes on to say in trust, *"For in God love is unfailing, and great is God's power to deliver."*

That, too, is said from the depths, and I suggest (and here I'm going out on a linguistic limb) that depths also stands for the deepest and firmest realities we know, the place where the great assurances as well as the great questions are found. If we identify with the writer's cry of affliction, maybe we can also identify with the writer's cry of affirmation. In both cases, we're in good company.

So I write you, Mackenzie, "out of the depths": out of both kinds of depths, the depths of fear and anguish, but also the depths of those things that endure—hope and trust and love. It's a tough balancing act between those two, but it's maybe the most important balancing act of all.

There's one other song in the songbook that has stood the test of time better than most of the others. It was played on a record in church last Sunday where we offered prayers for your recovery. I've been whispering some of its words to you for the last two weeks and I will continue to do so. You can't sing them for yourself yet, so I'll change the words a little and say them to you, words that are all about you. So we're in this together: I speak, you listen. We need each other. It's a great arrangement. (On the record we heard, Bobby McFerrin's version, the shepherd was a woman. Fair enough. In this letter, just to keep things balanced, I'll refer to the shepherd as "he," and we can discuss this matter when you reach the age of reason.)

Mackenzie, the Lord is your shepherd, your guardian. You shall not want for anything. He makes you lie down in green meadows, where you are nourished. He leads you beside still waters, where you may rest. *He revives your spirit.* Even when you walk through a valley of deep darkness, in the shadow of death (which is where you have been, Mackenzie), you need fear no evil, for God is with you always. *His shepherd's staff protects you.* God has anointed your head with blessing, and the cup of life overflows for you. Goodness and unfailing mercy will follow you all the days of your life, however short or long, and you will continue to dwell in God's house through all the years to come.

Amen and amen.

Notes

The following notes are included to help interested readers pursue certain themes of the sermons in more detail.

The biblical passages are usually quoted from *The Revised English Bible* (London: Oxford University Press and Cambridge University Press, 1989). Occasionally I have made my own adaptations, drawing on *The Oxford Annotated Bible: The Revised Standard Version* (London: Oxford University Press, 1965) and other translations, either to render the passage in inclusive language or to highlight a point central to the sermon. On a very few occasions I have retained the word "Lord," since I do not know another English word that does full justice to the Greek *Kyrios*.

Chapter 1. Mystery: Where Questions Count for More than Answers

The distinction between a mystery and a problem is further developed in Gabriel Marcel, *Being and Having* (Westminster: Dacre Press, 1949), 100–1, 116–22. On the theme of silence, see Dietrich Bonhoeffer, *Christ the Center* (New York: Harper & Row, 1978), and Gustavo Gutiérrez, *On Job: God-Talk and the Suffering of the Innocent* (Maryknoll, N.Y.: Orbis Books, 1987). The quotation on wonder is from Alice Walker, *The Color Purple* (New York: Washington Square Press, 1982), 247.

Chapter 2. Theology: Loving God with the Mind

The position developed in this chapter is by no means universally accepted. For followers of Karl Barth, for example, the starting point is never "where we are" but always the definitive revelation of God in Jesus Christ. This book as a whole safeguards that definitive revelation. Whether it becomes a reality first or last is not as important as that, by whatever route, we get to the place where we can freely affirm it for ourselves.

Chapter 3. Lost and Found: Grace, Amazing

A fuller treatment of grace as acceptance is found in Paul Tillich, *The Shaking of the Foundations* (London: SCM Press, 1949), especially the sermon "You Are Accepted." The text of "Amazing Grace," by John Newton, is as follows:

> Amazing grace, how sweet the sound,
> That saved a wretch like me!
> I once was lost, but now am found,
> Was blind, but now I see.
>
> 'Twas grace that taught my heart to fear,
> And grace my fears relieved;
> How precious did that grace appear
> The hour I first believed!
>
> Through many dangers, toils, and snares,
> I have already come;
> 'Tis grace has brought me safe thus far,
> And grace will lead me home.
>
> The Lord has promised good to me,
> His word my hope secures;
> He will my shield and portion be
> As long as life endures.
>
> When we've been there ten thousand years,
> Bright shining as the sun,
> We've no less days to sing God's praise
> Than when we'd first begun.

The excerpt from "For the Time Being" is in *The Collected Poetry of W. H. Auden* (New York: Random House, ©1945 W. H. Auden), 459.

Chapter 4. That Much-Abused Word "Love"

A helpful treatment of "Love and Law in Catholicism and Protestantism" is Reinhold Niebuhr's essay by that title in Robert McAfee Brown, ed., *The Essential Reinhold Niebuhr* (New Haven, Conn.: Yale University Press, 1986), chap. 11.

Chapter 5. Liberation: Cliché or Rediscovery?

The three levels of liberation in Christian thought are developed in more detail in Gustavo Gutiérrez, *A Theology of Liberation,* rev. ed. (Maryknoll, N.Y.: Orbis Books, 1988), 23–25, 204–5, 137; and in *The Truth Shall Make You Free* (Maryknoll, N.Y.: Orbis Books, 1990), pp. 121–24. I have summarized these discussions in *Gustavo Gutiérrez: An Introduction to Liberation Theology* (Maryknoll, N.Y.: Orbis Books, 1990), 104–6, 152–55. The South African Freedom Song is available with both words and music in Anders Nyberg, ed., *Freedom Is Coming* (Chapel Hill, N.C.: Walton, 1984).

Chapter 6. Reversals, Reversals, Reversals

I have dealt with the Isaiah/Luke passages in more detail in *Unexpected News: Reading the Bible with Third World Eyes* (Philadelphia: Westminster Press, 1984), chap. 6.

Chapter 7. Reconciliation: The Bottom Line

The full text of the 1967 Confession of Faith of the Presbyterian Church is available in Edward A. Dowey, *A Commentary on the Confession of 1967 and An Introduction to the Book of Confessions* (Philadelphia: Westminster Press, 1968).

Chapter 8. The Official and Unofficial Reports of a Lower Echelon Functionary in Herod's Court (Advent)

A fuller treatment of messianic hopes and expectations is found in Reinhold Niebuhr, *The Nature and Destiny of Man,* vol. 2 (New York: Charles Scribner's Sons, 1943), chaps. 1 and 2.

Chapter 9. Three Messengers (Which Is What the Greek Word *Angelos* Means) Discuss Past and Future Assignments (Epiphany)

We know virtually nothing with any certainty about the three kings. The legendary quality of the biblical reports invites poetic license to those who wish to build on them.

Chapter 10. The Biblical Obsession with Food (Ministry)

Positing a radical distinction between the sacred and the secular is perhaps the primal heresy. It is challenged here and elsewhere throughout the book.

Chapter 11. Mary and Martha: A Conundrum (Ministry)

My greatest helps in dealing with this difficult material were Carol A. Newsom and Sharon H. Ringe, eds., *The Women's Bible Commentary* (Louisville, Ky: Westminster/John Knox Press, 1992), especially Jane Schaberg's treatment of Luke, 275–92; and the treatment of the episode in Gustavo Gutiérrez, *The God of Life* (Maryknoll, N.Y.: Orbis Books,1991), 169–71. I feel duty-bound to report that when I voiced the proposal (in paragraph five) that Jesus, Mary, and Martha repair to the kitchen and talk there while helping to prepare the meal, a significant proportion of the congregation broke into applause.

Chapter 12. "So What Happened Next?" (The Transfiguration) A Dialogue Sermon with Sydney T. Brown

Some of this material is developed, in a different form, in my *Unexpected News: Reading the Bible with Third World Eyes,* chap. 8.

Chapter 13. Holy Week according to CBS and NPR, or Dan Rather and Robert MacNeil Cover the Jerusalem Beat (Palm Sunday and Good Friday)

All characters in this chapter are imaginary creations of the author. Any resemblance to persons living or dead, especially those with familiar names, is purely coincidental.

Chapter 14. The Life and Times of Old Tom Didymus (Easter)

Early church tradition assigned to the apostle Thomas the task of converting India. This tradition has been accepted here for purposes of completing the story of his life and death.

Chapter 15. The Apocryphal Council of Alexandria (Trinity Sunday)

The synonym for "apocryphal" is "fictitious." This may be helpful to perplexed readers, who should also be warned that the dialogue favors the Trinitarian formulation known as *modalistic monarchianism*. (This may not be helpful to perplexed readers.) All readers are urged to consult a reliable source such as Theodore Peters, *God as Trinity* (Louisville, Ky.: Westminster/John Knox Press, 1993). Discerning readers should also note an ambiguity in the last sentence of the introductory material, where it is not fully clear whether only the *minutes* of the council were lost "in the sands of Egypt during a purge of heretics," or whether the *participants* at the council suffered a similar fate.

Chapter 16. "How Shall We Sing the Lord's Song in a Strange Land?"

Few people have dealt more perceptively with memory as both a blessing and a curse than the novelist Elie Wiesel. See in particular *A Jew Today* (New York: Random House, 1978), esp. "The Scrolls, Too, Are Mortal"; *A Beggar in Jerusalem* (New York: Avon Books, 1970); *Souls on Fire* (New York: Random House, 1972), and *From the Kingdom of Memory* (New York: Summit Books, 1990).

Chapter 17. The Spiral of Violence

The "spiral of violence" is described in Dom Helder Câmara, *The Spiral of Violence* (Denville, Tex.: Dimension Books, 1971). I have expanded the theme in my *Religion and Violence*, 2d ed. (Philadelphia: Westminster Press, 1987), chap. 1, 8–12. "Come Lord" is quoted from Dom Helder Câmara, *The Desert Is Fertile*, trans. Francis McDonagh (Maryknoll, N.Y.: Orbis Books, 1981), 14.

Chapter 18. Sexuality and Homosexuality: A Problem for the Churches

On the textual intricacies of the early parts of Genesis, see the full treatment in E. A. Speiser, *Genesis*, The Anchor Bible (Garden City, N.Y.: Doubleday & Co., 1964), esp. the Introduction. There is an increasing literature on Christian faith and homosexuality. A recent treatment, well-written and well-documented, is Gary Comstock, *Gay Theology without Apology* (Cleveland: Pilgrim Press, 1993). On overall issues of sexuality and Christian faith, the writings of James Nelson are particularly helpful. See James B. Nelson, *Embodiment: An Approach to Sexuality and Christian Theology* (Minneapolis: Augsburg Publishing House, 1978); *Between Two Gardens: Reflections on Sexuality and Religious Experience* (New York: Pilgrim Press, 1983); and *Body Theology* (Louisville, Ky.: Westminster/John Knox Press, 1992), esp. chaps. 4 and 12.

Chapter 19. Scandal, Justice, Pearl Harbor, and Other Related Items, Including "a Refiner's Fire"

The occasion of this sermon was the fiftieth anniversary of Pearl Harbor. The concerns highlighted by that occasion have not ceased to be important.

Chapter 20. Sacrifice—and the Federal Budget

The term "preferential option for the poor" was discussed by the Latin American Roman Catholic bishops at a conference in Medellín, Colombia, in 1968, even though the phrase itself was not used. It was used, however, in their next conference at Puebla, Mexico, in 1979. John Eagleson and Philip Scharper, eds., *Puebla and Beyond* (Maryknoll, N.Y.: Orbis Books, 1979), 361, provides references. The theme figures strongly in the pastoral letter of the North American Roman Catholic Bishops, *Economic Justice for All* (Washington, D.C.: National Conference of Catholic Bishops, 1986). David O'Brien and Thomas Shannon, eds., *Catholic Social Thought* (Maryknoll, N.Y.: Orbis Books, 1992), is an excellent documentary of Catholic teaching on this and other matters. On overall issues see also J. Philip Wogaman, *Christian Ethics: A Historical Introduction* (Louisville, Ky.: Westminster/John Knox Press, 1993).

Chapter 21. Giving Thanks in the Midst of Death?

I am grateful to the members of Jim Burnett's family for granting permission to share this personal testimony, which was created chiefly with them in mind.

Chapter 22. Dear Mackenzie: A Letter from the Depths

In a shortened form, this sermon was published in *Christian Century*, March 2, 1994, 27–28. The Auden excerpt is from "Under Which Lyre," (Phi Beta Kappa Poem, Harvard, 1946), *Nones* (London: Faber and Faber, 1952), 62.